Criminal Justice: A Very Short Introduction

VERY SHORT INTRODUCTIONS are for anyone wanting a stimulating and accessible way into a new subject. They are written by experts, and have been translated into more than 40 different languages.

The series began in 1995, and now covers a wide variety of topics in every discipline. The VSI library now contains over 400 volumes—a Very Short Introduction to everything from Psychology and Philosophy of Science to American History and Relativity—and continues to grow in every subject area.

Very Short Introductions available now:

ACCOUNTING Christopher Nobes
ADVERTISING Winston Fletcher
AFRICAN AMERICAN RELIGION
    Eddie S. Glaude Jr.
AFRICAN HISTORY John Parker and
    Richard Rathbone
AFRICAN RELIGIONS Jacob K. Olupona
AGNOSTICISM Robin Le Poidevin
ALEXANDER THE GREAT
    Hugh Bowden
AMERICAN HISTORY Paul S. Boyer
AMERICAN IMMIGRATION
    David A. Gerber
AMERICAN LEGAL HISTORY
    G. Edward White
AMERICAN POLITICAL HISTORY
    Donald Critchlow
AMERICAN POLITICAL PARTIES
    AND ELECTIONS L. Sandy Maisel
AMERICAN POLITICS Richard M. Valelly
THE AMERICAN PRESIDENCY
    Charles O. Jones
THE AMERICAN REVOLUTION
    Robert J. Allison
AMERICAN SLAVERY
    Heather Andrea Williams
THE AMERICAN WEST Stephen Aron
AMERICAN WOMEN'S HISTORY
    Susan Ware
ANAESTHESIA Aidan O'Donnell
ANARCHISM Colin Ward
ANCIENT ASSYRIA Karen Radner
ANCIENT EGYPT Ian Shaw
ANCIENT EGYPTIAN ART AND
    ARCHITECTURE Christina Riggs

ANCIENT GREECE Paul Cartledge
THE ANCIENT NEAR EAST
    Amanda H. Podany
ANCIENT PHILOSOPHY Julia Annas
ANCIENT WARFARE Harry Sidebottom
ANGELS David Albert Jones
ANGLICANISM Mark Chapman
THE ANGLO-SAXON AGE John Blair
THE ANIMAL KINGDOM
    Peter Holland
ANIMAL RIGHTS David DeGrazia
THE ANTARCTIC Klaus Dodds
ANTISEMITISM Steven Beller
ANXIETY Daniel Freeman and
    Jason Freeman
THE APOCRYPHAL GOSPELS
    Paul Foster
ARCHAEOLOGY Paul Bahn
ARCHITECTURE Andrew Ballantyne
ARISTOCRACY William Doyle
ARISTOTLE Jonathan Barnes
ART HISTORY Dana Arnold
ART THEORY Cynthia Freeland
ASTROBIOLOGY David C. Catling
ATHEISM Julian Baggini
AUGUSTINE Henry Chadwick
AUSTRALIA Kenneth Morgan
AUTISM Uta Frith
THE AVANT GARDE David Cottington
THE AZTECS Davíd Carrasco
BACTERIA Sebastian G. B. Amyes
BARTHES Jonathan Culler
THE BEATS David Sterritt
BEAUTY Roger Scruton
BESTSELLERS John Sutherland

For more information visit our website

www.oup.com/vsi/

Julian V. Roberts

CRIMINAL JUSTICE

A Very Short Introduction

OXFORD
UNIVERSITY PRESS

OXFORD
UNIVERSITY PRESS

Great Clarendon Street, Oxford, OX2 6DP,
United Kingdom

Oxford University Press is a department of the University of Oxford.
It furthers the University's objective of excellence in research, scholarship,
and education by publishing worldwide. Oxford is a registered trade mark of
Oxford University Press in the UK and in certain other countries

© Julian V. Roberts 2015

The moral rights of the author have been asserted

First edition published in 2015

Impression: 1

Published in the United States of America by Oxford University Press
198 Madison Avenue, New York, NY 10016, United States of America

British Library Cataloguing in Publication Data

Data available

Library of Congress Control Number: 2015934241

ISBN 978-0-19-871649-5

Printed in Great Britain by
Ashford Colour Press Ltd, Gosport, Hampshire

Links to third party websites are provided by Oxford in good faith and
for information only. Oxford disclaims any responsibility for the materials
contained in any third party website referenced in this work.

For M. G.

Contents

Contents

Preface

Writing any Very Short Introduction is challenging to academics used to the relative luxury of 100,000-word volumes and able to qualify (and nuance) their judgements with pages of footnotes. A volume on criminal justice is particularly difficult as the theory, structure, and practice of criminal justice varies greatly around the world and across the common–civil law divide. Even within the common law world, criminal justice looks very different when comparing, for example, California and Cardiff. In addition, scholarship on criminal justice is infused with ideology and opinion. Many scholars have fixed views on issues such as the death penalty or the role of the victim. Two causes of this intransigence are the limitations of the research in criminal justice and the politicized nature of the subject. Empirical research has been unable to generate definitive answers to many of the critical questions in criminal justice, although the evidence base is growing constantly. We can draw some reasonably confident conclusions about what works and where the problems (and solutions) lie. I have tried to reflect consensual positions on controversial issues and to encapsulate the latest research findings. In light of the many elements and stages of criminal justice, I have had to be selective, as any given chapter can address only a limited number of issues. Wherever I cite a statistic from a particular jurisdiction, I use one representative of several countries. From time to time, I note the degree to which criminal justice policies and practices conflict with public opinion, or areas where public perceptions of criminal justice are strikingly at odds with reality. My goal is to introduce key elements of the criminal justice system to readers. The best introduction to criminal justice, however, is to attend a busy criminal court—and watch the drama unfold.

Acknowledgements

I am grateful to Andrea Keegan, Jenny Nugee, Carrie Hickman, and Joy Mellor from the Oxford University Press; two anonymous reviewers; Professor Candace McCoy (John Jay College of Criminal Justice); as well as the following colleagues and friends who provided helpful comments on earlier drafts: Judge Patrick Healy (Quebec Court of Justice), Dr Marie Manikis (Faculty of Law, McGill University), Dr Chris Giacomantonio (Rand Europe), Professor Ralph Henham (Nottingham Trent School of Law), Professor Barry Mitchell (School of Law, Coventry University), Umar Azmeh (Barrister, Middle Temple). I am particularly indebted to George Millenbach, a scholar and a gentleman residing in New York City.

Julian V. Roberts
Worcester College, Oxford
1 January 2015

List of illustrations

Chapter 1
Introducing criminal justice

Society causes crime and creates offenders. Think of Robinson Crusoe on the island, but without his 'Man Friday'. On a desert island there's no-one from whom to steal, no-one to assault. No society, no laws, no crime, and no criminals. Once a society emerges, rules develop, and when they are broken society must respond—otherwise the rules would lose their potency to affect behaviour.

Modern societies have evolved principles which guide the decision to criminalize specific acts (or failures to act). The philosopher John Stuart Mill argued that conduct must infringe some important social value—for example, another person's freedom or security—before the State classifies the act as an offence. Most systems of justice try to restrict their application to more serious forms of misconduct. In an ideal world, merely labelling theft a crime may be sufficient to prevent one person appropriating another's property. In the real world, however, this alone will not prevent the crime. So society imposes a *disincentive* to offend: people who violate the law will be subject to prosecution and punishment.

In order to prosecute and punish people who violate its laws, the State needs a criminal justice system (hereafter CJS) in which the professionals have a wide range of potential responses. A police officer may simply caution a person. At the other end of the spectrum, some CJSs go so far as to execute offenders. The range of response is necessary because the sort of law-breaking varies enormously, from trivial acts through to crimes which result in the loss of life. Offenders vary too: the same crime might be committed by people in very different circumstances. If a person intentionally takes the life of another without legal excuse this constitutes murder, yet if one case involves a woman who kills her suffering and terminally ill husband while the other was a contract killing, the two offenders will be punished in different ways—and for good reason. The harm is the same—the loss of human life—but the offender's motives (and hence level of culpability) differ enormously. Both offenders may be guilty of the same crime (murder), but they will spend very different amounts of time in prison.

The objectives of criminal justice

Public institutions such as hospitals or the army have clear mandates: to improve the health of the nation and to protect national security, respectively; the mission of the CJS is more complicated. For example, some people argue that countries with private and public hospitals should adopt a single public health system. Ultimately, however, all medical professionals should share the same goal—that patient care is paramount. The patient is at the heart of health care, but the victim is not always the focus of the CJS. Criminal proceedings typically begin when a victim reports a crime to the police, yet this does not mean that the CJS is exclusively or primarily about victim welfare. As a case moves through the criminal process—from arrest through to trial and the imposition of sentence—a range of decisions will be made. The professionals making these decisions balance the interests of the victim, the due process rights of the defendant, the broader public interest, as well as considerations of cost effectiveness. The system has multiple (and potentially conflicting) objectives. The distinction between punishment and prevention is a good example of the potential conflicts in criminal justice.

Punishing and preventing crime

Punishing the offender is only one goal of criminal justice, and even this aim encompasses several purposes. For example, a legal punishment may reinforce individual morality: we report income to the tax authorities in part because we regard it as wrong to do otherwise. Hearing about the punishments imposed on tax dodgers reinforces this sense of morality. Punishment may also prevent crime—whether by the offender who has just been caught or by other individuals tempted to follow his example (since 95 per cent of people charged with an offence are male, throughout this book I will use the male pronoun). Rehabilitating the offender is another important goal of criminal justice: what can the State do to address the causes of the offender's criminal behaviour—helping with his drug abuse problem, for example? Or the CJS may decide that the offender is too dangerous to be released back into the community and should be detained indefinitely: crime prevention through *incapacitation* of the offender.

It is better to prevent than to treat or punish after the fact, whether we are talking about disease or crime. Crime prevention involves far more than the CJS; indeed, attempting to prevent crime through the application of criminal justice alone is a policy doomed to failure. Many agencies and systems outside the CJS contribute to crime prevention. Mental health services, school programmes, and community agencies all play a key role in preventing crime.

Despite its importance, prevention strategies generally take a back seat to punishment as a way of preventing crime. The courts and prisons account for a much larger slice of the criminal justice budget than crime prevention programmes, yet community-based prevention programmes offer better value for money in terms of the volume of crimes prevented. Crime prevention initiatives which improve social conditions, or increase the opportunities for law abiding citizens, are more effective in preventing crime than are prison sentences for convicted offenders.

Making it harder to steal a car, break into a home, or rob a bank is more effective in preventing car theft, burglary, or robbery than putting more police onto the streets or sending burglars to prison for longer periods. Bank robbery is a good example of the crime prevention strategy known as '*target-hardening*'. Such robberies have declined by over 90 per cent in the UK over the past twenty years, with similar trends in other countries. This is due to enhanced security in banks, including self-locking cash drawers and vaults and silent alarms, rather than being due to any changes in the number of police or severity of sentences for bank robbery. Car thefts have dropped almost as rapidly in countries where vehicles with more secure locks are standard equipment. Simply put, it is much harder to rob a bank or steal a car today compared to fifty years ago; so fewer robberies and thefts are committed.

Offenders follow opportunities, and many of the traditional sources of acquisitive crime have dried up. Instead, the Internet has become the focus of much criminality—the potential profits are immense and the network is poorly regulated. Few Internet crimes are detected; fewer still result in prosecution and punishment. Preventing crime in this new domain is probably the single greatest challenge to domestic and international criminal justice.

Crime prevention assumes many forms and functions both within and beyond the CJS. Situational crime prevention occurs within the CJS. There are three kinds of situational crime prevention. One involves *increasing the effort* that offenders must spend to commit a crime. Steering wheel locks, enhanced security barriers, and sophisticated locks for property and gun control involving time-consuming registration are examples of this form of crime prevention. *Increasing the risks* of detection is a second approach.

More police patrols, more frequent or intrusive searches of persons at border controls, and enhanced baggage screening are all strategies which raise the likelihood of apprehending an offender. Finally, many businesses have *reduced the rewards* gained by criminal behaviour by lowering the amount of cash or valuables held in a facility.

Of course, it's easier to punish than to prevent but the re-offending rates demonstrate that criminal justice punishments are often unsuccessful. Most offenders sent to prison will re-offend, because prison fails to correct the problems that caused the offending. The public are well aware of the limitations of the CJS in this regard. When asked to rate the job that the CJS is doing, the public give the system high marks for treating people fairly, but low marks for reducing the level of crime in society or stopping offenders from re-offending.

Key principles of criminal justice

Several key principles guide the practice of criminal justice in Western nations. First, criminal prosecution should remain a last resort—the CJS should prosecute an individual or a company only when all other remedies have failed or are deemed inappropriate. The consequences of this principle are two-fold. First, the legislature should criminalize only conduct which is sufficiently serious as to justify criminal sanctions; and, second, the potentially serious consequences for convicted offenders mean that prosecution should occur only when other interventions—for example, warnings and cautions—are inadequate.

The second principle is that criminal justice interventions should be the minimal response necessary. If a warning is sufficient to recall the offender to law abiding society, don't charge him with an offence. If a fine is sufficient punishment for the crime, don't send him to prison. Sometimes this is referred to as the principle of *penal restraint*.

In determining the level of State intervention and punishment the CJS should be guided by the principle of *proportionality*. The severity of the criminal justice response should increase as the crime becomes more serious. The more important the rule, the more serious the consequences for the State when people violate the rule. 'Thou shall not kill' is a more important rule than 'Thou shalt not steal'. The State therefore imposes more severe penalties upon people who break the more important rules, or laws. At least that is the theory. In practice, things turn out differently. Over the years, many forms of trivial misconduct—or matters of morality rather than harm to society—have become subject to criminal penalties. For example, should assisting a person to commit suicide be a crime when taking one's own life is not an offence? Should it be an offence to provide sexual services in return for money? Should it be a crime to pay someone to have sex? Or is this just an example of legal moralism?

In reality, prosecutions are sometimes launched in cases where there seems no public interest in proceeding. A good example of inappropriate charging occurred in England in 2014. A local prosecutor had a rush of blood to the head and charged three homeless people with taking food that had been thrown away by a supermarket. Thankfully, the intervention of the supermarket chain and a senior prosecutor resulted in the charges being dropped.

The level of CJS intervention frequently exceeds that which is necessary, and penalties are often imposed in flagrant violation of proportionality at sentencing. Still, it's good to keep these guiding principles in mind.

Models of criminal justice

Once a victim reports a crime, the State police may initiate an investigation which can lead to the prosecution of a suspect. In order to collect evidence and to determine whether a specific person is guilty of the alleged crime, the system needs a set of rules of procedure; it needs an operational model.

CJSs vary widely but they generally fall into one of two contrasting models: the *adversarial model* and the *inquisitorial model*. An adversarial criminal justice proceeding involves two parties: the State (represented by a prosecutor) and the individual against whom the State has laid a criminal charge. The person accused of a crime is usually represented by a lawyer, his own or one appointed by the State. In recent years, with cutbacks to legal aid in many countries, an increasing number of defendants elect to represent themselves, without a lawyer. This is regrettable; the consequences of a conviction are so significant that defendants should always have the benefit of professional advice.

If the accused denies the charge, a trial will be held where the two adversaries present their case. The presiding judge seldom intervenes as the parties present their case, interrupting proceedings only if there is a danger of injustice. This model is followed in the common law world, which includes all English-speaking nations, particularly commonwealth countries.

In contrast, the inquisitorial model relies on an investigating judge who launches the investigation and actively guides the actions of the police in collecting evidence. This judge will identify and interview witnesses and eventually conduct the trial. Most European countries like France and Italy follow this model. In France, the investigating and presiding judge is called the *juge d'instruction*. Another way of distinguishing the two systems is to see the adversarial system as 'lawyer-led'—the course of the case is determined by the actions of the two parties—the State prosecutor and the lawyer for the defendant. In contrast, the inquisitorial model is 'judge-led'—with developments unfolding according to the judge's directions.

A good example of the contrasting approaches involves the question of previous convictions. A defendant now charged with robbery has three prior convictions for robbery and assault. Should these earlier crimes—for which the accused has already been punished—be brought to the attention of the court deciding whether he is guilty of this latest robbery? The adversarial model generally prevents the trial judge or jury (if the case is being tried before a jury) from hearing about these prior convictions. The reason for this is that a jury composed of members of the public without legal training may be tempted to conclude 'he's done it before, so he must have done it this time'. So long as the defendant elects not to testify—he is under no obligation to do so under this system—any prior convictions will usually remain unknown to the judge unless and until the defendant is convicted.

In contrast, in the inquisitorial model of justice the court will learn of the accused's prior crimes. The system assumes that the judges, or the mixed panel of judges and laypersons, will decide the current case on its merits and not be unduly influenced by the previous convictions. This is an unwise assumption; research suggests that hearing about a defendant's prior convictions can be highly prejudicial. People tend to infer guilt directly upon hearing of the offender's previous convictions.

Is one model of criminal justice superior? It's a hard question to answer; comparative research suggests that the adversarial model is better at uncovering the facts about the crime. The adversarial model also has more protections for the person accused of a crime; under the inquisitorial model there is an assumption that the judge will act appropriately and that such protections are less necessary. Litigants—people going through the system as defendants facing a charge—seem to prefer the adversarial model, but no definitive comparison of the two systems of criminal justice has been conducted. However, there are costs associated with the adversarial approach, not least of which is the diminished role of the crime victim.

Victims play a greater role in the inquisitorial systems of justice. Adversarial justice has long been criticized for ignoring the interests of the victim, although victims now have more rights at, and influence over, a criminal prosecution in adversarial systems of justice. Finally, it would be wrong to assume that adversarial justice is fixed in time and across jurisdictions. Criminal justice varies greatly across different Western nations. It has evolved greatly over the centuries and continues to evolve. The adversarial trial in particular has changed; Western criminal justice has become less adversarial. The victim now has more influence and in this sense criminal justice has become more like the continental systems.

Components of criminal justice

We call it a 'system', but the CJS is better described as a collection of inter-related, yet independent, branches. The components of criminal justice include police, prosecution, judiciary, prisons, probation, and parole. Each branch or agency has a specific mandate and particular profile of professionals. The police aim to protect the public; the courts ensure that in protecting the public and prosecuting accused persons, important due process requirements are met; the prisons and parole agencies administer punishments in a way that is intended to deter, reform, and provide justice.

All branches of criminal justice are assisted by a wide range of ancillary services and professionals: victims' services work with the police; probation with the courts; and so forth. A diverse collection of private and public service providers help to manage and supervise offenders in the community or to provide services in prisons. The conflicting mandates of different branches of criminal justice can sometimes cause problems. The police are often critical of judges who release the accused on bail when the police have opposed bail. Or take sentencing and parole. At sentencing, a court is concerned with imposing a sentence which corresponds to the seriousness of the crime; however, when determining whether to grant or deny release on parole, parole boards are more concerned about the risk the prisoner may pose to the community, and whether release will promote his rehabilitation. Sometimes a long sentence of imprisonment therefore translates into a relatively short term of imprisonment, because the parole board has released the prisoner early, believing him to be a low risk to society, despite his having been imprisoned for committing a quite serious crime.

Public perceptions

Researchers in many countries have explored the perceptions of the public. It is important to know what the public think about criminal justice professionals—if people have little confidence in the CJS they are unlikely to co-operate as witnesses, or serve as jurors. After decades of surveys we now know a lot about the views of the public. In conjunction with colleagues in the UK, Canada, and the US, I have explored public attitudes to police, courts, and corrections. Our surveys often ask the public to rate various branches of criminal justice, or to express how much confidence they have in different criminal justice professionals such as the police or prosecutors. A clear hierarchy of confidence emerges: the public have most confidence in the police, least confidence in judges and parole boards. In the UK, three-quarters of the public in 2010 expressed confidence in the police; less than half the survey sample had confidence in the prisons. Similar trends can be seen in all other Western countries.

One reason for our greater trust and confidence in the police is mere familiarity: we see police officers on a daily basis, in uniform or in marked cars. Other criminal justice professionals tend to be less visible. When was the last time you saw a judge or a prosecutor at work? The public also know more about the work of the police. When a survey asked people to state how much they knew about various criminal justice professionals, three-quarters said they knew a lot about the police, while only one-quarter had as much knowledge of the prosecution branch of the justice system. The mandates of the various branches of criminal justice also play a role: the police are seen as fighting crime; parole boards are seen as helping offenders (by letting them out before their terms of imprisonment end). This aligns the police more closely with the public.

One blind spot for many members of the public concerns the limited ability of the CJS to meet our expectations: most people don't realize that there are sound restrictions on the powers of the CJS as well as limits on its ability to prevent crime.

Limits on the power of the CJS

If the State allowed itself unlimited powers to investigate, prosecute, and punish suspected offenders, we might all be constantly under suspicion. If arrested, we would struggle to defend ourselves—especially in light of the vast resources that the CJS can mobilize. This state of affairs may suit a totalitarian regime, but in liberal democracies we are uncomfortable with such an arrangement, and have set important limits on the power of the CJS.

For example, the police are not allowed to eavesdrop on our phone calls without prior authorization from a judge. (Whether the security services do so anyway is another matter.) Similarly, if you are charged with a criminal offence, the prosecutor cannot spring the case against you on the first day of trial: you (and your lawyer) need to know the evidence against you in advance. In this way you can prepare your defence—or have sufficient awareness of the State's case for you to decide whether to plead guilty. If brought to trial, you cannot be compelled to testify against your will. It is a general requirement of criminal justice that the State must prove both that the defendant committed the relevant act (or, more rarely, failed to take some action) and that he had the necessary state of mind to do so at the time. In addition, the prosecution has the burden of proving each element of the offence 'beyond a reasonable doubt'.

These limits on the powers of criminal justice professionals are often referred to as *due process* protections. The State should prosecute only in accordance with the principles of due process. If it violates these principles, the court will intervene. Imagine that following an unauthorized search of your home the police find evidence which is then used to prosecute you. If the court accepts that the search was illegal, the evidence will normally be excluded. If that is the only evidence against you, the court will order an end to the State's prosecution. The evidence may conclusively demonstrate that you have committed a crime—but if it was illegally gathered, you're off the hook: 'Police error in your favour, do not go directly to jail'.

CJSs seek a balance between *due process* considerations and the need for effective *crime control*. The distinction between these two opposing poles was popularized by Herbert Packer in the 1960s. If crime control is pursued to the exclusion of all other considerations, the system would have too much power and we would be forever looking over our shoulders. On the other hand, if we place too many due process restrictions on the power of the police or the prosecution this will increase the number of offenders who manage to evade justice. It's a question of achieving the right balance—the pursuit of crime control while respecting reasonable limits on the power of the police, the courts, and the other branches of criminal justice.

A degree of balance is also necessary in terms of the discretion allowed criminal justice professionals.

Discretion in criminal justice decision-making

The most important element of criminal justice is the discretion that professionals exercise. This is a finely balanced issue, like many others in the field of criminal justice. Too much discretion increases the risk of discrimination and disparity of treatment. Judges who have wide discretion and little guidance as to how to exercise that discretion will impose sentences which vary greatly. On the other hand, when discretion is removed entirely, another form of injustice occurs. Mandatory sentencing laws are a good example. These laws, which have proliferated across the US and other nations, require judges to impose the same sentence on all offenders convicted of a particular crime—regardless of their individual circumstances. A good example of this is a case in the UK in which the offender was convicted of possession of a prohibited weapon (a shotgun). This offence carries a mandatory sentence of five years' imprisonment. That may not sound unreasonable as a sentence, but this individual only came to the attention of the CJS because he had been admitted to hospital after trying to kill himself with his (illegal) firearm. The court had no choice but to impose the sentence of several years in prison—a clearly unjust result arising from the removal of judicial discretion.

A just system will provide guidance for all actors in the criminal process—police, prosecutors, judges, probation officers, and parole boards—while allowing them to tailor their decisions to reflect the characteristics of individual offenders.

Limits on the effectiveness of criminal justice

Most people look to the CJS to prevent crime, yet the most important causes of crime, as well as the remedies for those causes, lie outside the scope of the system. Consider late night public disorder. Pubs in England used to close at the same time every night, spilling hundreds (or, in larger cities, thousands) of drunken revellers into the city centre at exactly the same time. Even tranquil university towns like Oxford resembled a scene from the movie *Animal House*—but with flying bottles and fists instead of food. The congregation of large numbers of young adults, many of whom are drunk, generates crime. One busy defence lawyer once remarked that if alcohol were to be prohibited, his criminal practice would dry up overnight. He was right: alcohol is the single most important source of business for the CJS. In England and Wales, alcohol or drugs were responsible for approximately a million crimes in 2014.

Some of this alcohol-fuelled criminality can be reduced by more (and better) policing, and by court-imposed restrictions on offenders convicted of drink-related crimes. However, the solutions ultimately lie in better regulation of alcohol sales (including minimum pricing and disincentives to over-consume); improved alcohol awareness education in schools; more sophisticated licensing hour arrangements; and other interventions that lie outside the CJS. As a society, however, we tend to see crime and disorder as problems that can be solved by more police, more prosecutions, and harsher punishments.

Another important limit on the CJS concerns the attrition of cases (or *case attrition*) through the system. Offenders appearing for sentence represent the tip of the proverbial iceberg—a very small percentage of all perpetrators. Of all crimes committed, only about 10 per cent are reported to the police. Victims may not want to get involved with the CJS—because the crime was a personal matter or not that serious, or because the victim thought the police could or would do nothing about it. Bike theft is a daily hazard for many Oxford residents. When my bike was stolen last year, I didn't report the theft because there was little the police could do to recover it. Some victims of much more serious crimes don't report them to the police because they worry about not being believed. This has long been the case for victims of rape and other sexual crimes. Surveys of crime victims generally find that less than one sexual assault in twenty is reported to the police, often for this reason.

Of all crimes, then, only some will come to the attention of the police. Of those crimes that are reported, the police will only be able to act on a minority—many cases will be dropped for various reasons such as the police decide no crime was actually committed. Once a charge is laid, some accused persons will drop out of the system because of problems with the prosecution's case, leading to the charges being stayed (in other words, withdrawn). And some offenders will be acquitted. It has been estimated by researchers that a sentence is imposed in only about 3 per cent of all crimes. That means that the vast majority of offenders remain unpunished.

This phenomenon of case attrition surprises many people. But why is it important? If courts deal with only a very small percentage of all offenders, whatever the court does to this small number will have little effect on *overall* crime rates. Expecting courts to control crime or reduce the overall levels of crime in society is akin to expecting surgery to control or reduce the incidence of coronary disease. Surgeons are adept at correcting the small number of cases that enter the operating theatre; and judges can impose proportionate sentences on the small percentage of offenders that appear for sentence. But heart disease and crime are best tackled in the community, by addressing the causes of coronary problems and criminal behaviour. If we can agree that the most important goal of criminal justice is to prevent crime, we should look not to the courts but to earlier stages of criminal justice, and indeed outside the CJS. Crime prevention is more effectively achieved by programmes in society, better (and more) police and related initiatives, than by changing the policies which affect only the small percentage of offenders who end up being sentenced.

Finally, however, we should not leave this introduction to the CJS without noting its failures.

Criminal *in*justice

Injustice occurs in many ways. Innocent people may be charged and even convicted of crimes they did not commit—wrongful convictions. Guilty parties may evade punishment entirely—wrongful acquittals.

Offenders may be punished more or less than they deserve—over- or under-punishment. Offenders from different racial or ethnic backgrounds may be treated more harshly—discrimination.

Wrongful convictions have generally been considered the worst form of injustice: the prospect of an innocent person languishing in prison seems worse to most people than that of the offender remaining at liberty for the crime. This issue is discussed further in Chapter 2.

Discrimination is one of the worst forms of criminal injustice. In every country a minority group (or groups) account for disproportionate numbers in criminal justice statistics. The group is usually a visible or ethnic minority: Black Americans; Aboriginal Canadians and Australians; Maoris in New Zealand. These populations account for a higher proportion of arrests, convictions, and prison admissions than would be expected on the basis of their numbers in the general population. One explanation is that these groups have suffered economic and social exclusion, and their social conditions have created the conditions for crime. However, higher rates of actual offending are only part of the story.

Discrimination at various stages of the CJS also plays a role. The police are more likely to concentrate their resources in neighbourhoods with high crime rates. When these areas also have a higher proportion of minority residents, the police will inevitably stop more minority citizens. The neighbourhood generates crime through a complex set of reasons such as poverty, unemployment, and drug use. It then attracts more police and the result is a higher rate of minority groups in the criminal justice statistics. Discrimination can take many forms; visible minority prisoners can be subject to racial abuse by staff or can be less likely to be released on parole.

The CJS pays more attention to some forms of crime than others. In an ideal world, the CJS would concentrate its resources to focus on the more serious crimes. The investment of time and resources would reflect the seriousness of the crime. In practice certain forms of offending attract disproportionate attention from the CJS. Crimes generally come to the attention of the police and result in official action following a report by a victim. The consequence is that some crimes—for example, against the institutionalized, the isolated elderly, and the environment—remain off the CJS radar screen. The so-called 'white collar' crimes—committed in boardrooms and by wealthy individuals—are greatly under-reported and seldom prosecuted. Deciding which cases to investigate and which to prosecute is often a discretionary decision taken by the police or the prosecution.

So much for the preliminaries. From here we will work through the criminal justice process, beginning with the police and ending back where the CJS begins—with the crime victim.

Chapter 2
Between the crime and the court

After the commission of the crime and prior to the accused entering a plea, the case is in the hands of the police and the prosecution branches of criminal justice. Most countries operate a professional and independent prosecution service—known as the Crown Prosecution Service in England and Wales. Maintaining a separate prosecution service permits some distance and independence from the professionals gathering evidence, namely the police.

Public vs private policing

Public policing is a relatively new component of criminal justice. Two centuries ago there were no State police at all; footpads, brigands, and robbers roamed freely across town and country. More recently, policing has become increasingly privatized. Today, vast areas of society are policed by private companies—including shopping malls, housing estates, schools, and universities. There are several reasons for this increased level of private security and police.

First, larger and larger areas of urban centres have become privatized so the public police have no jurisdiction. The so-called 'gated communities' are a good example of private security assuming a role that a century ago would have been the exclusive domain of the public police forces. Second, growing dissatisfaction with the level of protection provided by the public police has stimulated the market for private security firms. Third, the rapid expansion of surveillance technologies has meant that private security can offer homeowners a range of protections unavailable from their local police force. This increased use of private 'police' worries some criminal justice scholars; private security firms are not as accountable as the public police.

It is hard to capture the essentials of police work because policing varies enormously around the world. For example, in some countries officers carry firearms; elsewhere only specialized officers do so. Certain characteristics are common and one is that the police serve as a gatekeeper to the criminal justice system (CJS). If they do not act on a crime report, the incident will not enter the official statistics.

The police are usually the first contact with the CJS, whether for the victim, a witness, or a suspect, and the police response shapes all subsequent decisions in the CJS. The nature of this interaction with victims, witnesses, and offenders affects attitudes towards the entire CJS. Contact with the police can be either voluntary or involuntary, and the outcome negative or positive. Research reveals an interesting asymmetry: where an encounter has been negative (e.g., the police are disrespectful or aggressive), there is a strong—adverse—effect on perceptions of the whole CJS. On the other hand, where an interaction has been neutral, or even positive, perceptions of the system are less affected.

One of the most controversial policing practices is that of 'stop and search'. All police forces have the power to stop and search people, although the extent of the power and the legal regimes which regulate the practice vary. The common phrase used to justify an officer stopping a member of the public is that there are 'reasonable grounds for suspecting' that evidence of relevant offences will be found as a result of the search. The powers of the police are defined by a statute—for example, the Police and Criminal Evidence Act in England. However, like so many decisions in criminal justice, this one is subject to the exercising of discretion, and as such, it is applied more frequently against certain groups of people.

The police stop visible minorities more often than other citizens. This tendency has been well documented in the US, the UK, Canada, and other countries. In England, over one-quarter of the people stopped and searched by the police in 2014 were Black or Asian—despite these groups accounting for only 10 per cent of the population. A person from a Black ethnic group was much more likely to be stopped and searched than a White individual and also more likely to be arrested. In the US, Black drivers are much more likely to believe they had been stopped because of their race. Not surprisingly, surveys of the public reveal that visible minorities in both countries were less likely to see the police as constituting a legitimate authority.

The data on police stop and search practices are worrying from another perspective as well. Recent research in the US has demonstrated what are termed 'labelling' effects: juveniles who are frequently stopped and/or arrested are more likely to subsequently commit more serious acts of delinquency. The criminal justice intervention—stopping and searching or arresting an individual—has adverse effects that can be seen at a later date, showing that, paradoxically, it may contribute to, rather than prevent, crime.

Does stopping people on the street in this way actually result in arrests or prevent crime? There isn't much research into the crime preventative effects of 'stop, question, frisk' (SQF) policing, as this strategy is known in the US. The New York police seem to believe SQF works, but researchers disagree. Critics of the practice note that only a very small percentage of all stops result in arrest. Since the police need reasonable cause to stop a citizen in the first place, why is the subsequent arrest rate so low? In the UK, only about one stop in ten results in an arrest. This statistic raises questions about the legitimacy of the remaining 90 per cent of stops. Advocates of the practice argue that it has a deterrent effect, but the evidence is unconvincing. There are also likely to be *displacement* effects: if the police blitz a particular area and crime goes down, is this because potential offenders have been deterred or have they simply moved to another neighbourhood? Drug dealing is a good example. Street drug dealers are particularly agile in their response to policing initiatives. When the police move in, they move out, seeking clients in greener pastures where the police are less likely to be encountered.

Policing is increasingly a question of technology, with closed circuit television (CCTV) being a prime example. Private security firms are responsible for most of these surveillance systems. The public police have also turned to technology to assist their work. For example, portable video headgear or body-worn cameras can provide a permanent record of encounters with the public. This can assist in proving (or disproving) allegations of misconduct by police. It can also serve as a deterrent to misconduct; police officers are unlikely to break the rules in arresting a suspect when they know their actions are being recorded.

Officers spend a lot more time acquiring and using information from police databases, and this inevitably means less time engaged in more traditional 'street patrolling'. One consequence of this increased attention to mass information has been the development of areas dubbed 'hotspots'—areas of the city where particular crimes or offenders congregate. Clusters of addresses may constitute an area with an elevated risk of crime; this information can then be used to deploy police resources efficiently. One potential danger with this approach is that the enhanced police attention to certain areas or hotspots means that residents of these areas are subject to more attention from the police. This in turn can result in them being more likely to be arrested and then prosecuted.

Police practices have evolved considerably in recent years. Traditional policing involved a combination of routine and random patrols to prevent crime by maintaining a visible police presence in the streets, accompanied by a rapid response to calls for assistance from victims or witnesses to a crime. This approach to policing has proved to be at best inefficient, at worst unsuccessful—at least in terms of reducing crime. One reason for abandoning the approach is the recognition that crime is not a general phenomenon smoothly distributed across, say, a city. Drug dealers or juvenile gangs have a deleterious impact on a small number of neighbourhoods while residents of other areas of the same city are often unaware of these activities. Crime tends to be concentrated in certain areas, and the police response must reflect this reality. Even a rapid response—with police cars flying through the streets, sirens blaring—is ineffective. Speed of response is critical in medical emergencies: saving minutes saves lives. However, whether the police arrive on the scene of a crime in 5 minutes or in 50, it makes far less difference in terms of arrest rates and crime reduction.

On the other hand, one conventional or traditional police practice, that of foot patrols, does seem beneficial in terms of enhancing public confidence in the police. When the police patrol in this fashion they are more visible to the general public, and this visibility promotes reassurance that crime and antisocial behaviour are being moderated.

Otherwise, traditional approaches to policing have largely been discredited and replaced by tactics and strategies based upon crime data. 'Crime-mapping', for example, is used, whereby detailed maps of city neighbourhoods are drawn up based on a range of specific indicators. The result is a profile of crime hotspots in that city—an example of today's more focused approach to policing.

A range of more modern strategies have been developed, including:

- Offence-specific units: for example, units whose focus is on crime generated by, say, juvenile gangs or drug offenders. These units are manned by specialist officers who have specific skills and experience, gained by remaining in the unit for many years.

- Community-based policing: this broad strategy lays emphasis on engaging the community rather than simply policing the area. This can mean a range of initiatives, from officers making and maintaining links with community groups, to opening mini police stations in shopping malls. Small, 'pop-up' police stations help to break down the barrier between the police and the community which predominates when the police are based in large (and usually forbidding) police stations.

- Problem-solving policing: the idea here is that rather than just arresting people (sometimes repeatedly as they are then bailed and return to the area in which they were arrested), police officers engage with what is perceived to be causing a repeat crime problem.

These strategies promote a more scientific approach to the deployment of resources and the police response to crime and disorder.

Gun crime—a problem which is largely found in the US—is a good example of the way that targeted policing can work. One approach to reducing the frequency of gun-related crime is to impose a mandatory sentence of custody on all offenders carrying, or using, an illegal firearm to commit an offence. This is an expensive response (as are all criminal justice initiatives involving prison).

In contrast, targeted policing is more effective: when the police focus on illegal gun carrying in specific areas, the benefits in terms of reducing the number of firearms offences are clear.

Fix those windows! 'Broken windows'

Perhaps the most researched topic in policing is the so-called 'broken windows' theory. This theory proposes that disordered neighbourhoods attract offending. Once an area reveals signs of negligence—such as shattered windows, but also derelict buildings, graffiti, and abandoned cars—law-abiding residents tend to flee to more salubrious parts of the town or city. Gangs, drug dealers, and street prostitutes then move in—and the neighbourhood becomes criminalized. This theory has important consequences for policing. The argument is that early police intervention before a community reaches this state will prevent more (and more serious) offending. This approach to policing is sometimes called 'order maintenance policing', and a classic example of the use of this approach to policing can be found in New York City (NYC).

Beginning in 1994, the New York Police Department (NYPD) aggressively enforced misdemeanour laws against loitering and fare-dodging in the subway. Within a few years, the crime rate had declined significantly. Order maintenance policing, based on the 'broken windows' theory, was claimed to be responsible for this rare success story in criminal justice: 'no pane, no gain', we could say. Consequently, many researchers have been prompted to try to determine how much of the decline in crime in NYC was directly linked to this new approach to policing. However, the results have not been conclusive. And while research in criminal justice seldom generates definitive conclusions, research suggests that this kind of policing was not in fact responsible for the decline in crime rates—despite community residents reporting that they felt less afraid of crime when this approach was adopted. The reason this striking decline in crime rates in NYC cannot be explained by the city's approach to policing is simply that many other cities in the Western world have experienced similar declines in crime rates—and they have not all deployed this same approach to crime.

Increased powers of the police

The most radical change to police practices involves their additional powers. Instead of simply maintaining order and assisting in the prosecution of a case (by interviewing potential witnesses) in many countries the police now play a quasi-judicial role. They issue cautions and administer a range of responses which forestall, in the first instance at least, further State action. In fact, there is a wide range of options available to police when confronted with a person suspected of committing a crime. The police can: take no action or simply warn the individual; issue fixed penalty notices or official cautions, usually with conditions attached; or refer the person to a mediation programme which will involve the victim.

Research into policing strategies and tactics has revealed the limits on even the most effective approaches. The striking decline in crime rates across all Western nations since the mid-1990s has generated a great deal of scholarship. The exact causes of the drop in crime rates remain obscure, but it seems unlikely that more effective policing has been responsible. While police practices vary considerably around the world, all countries have experienced a relatively similar decline in crime. There is a broader lesson here. Criminal justice policies vary enormously around the world: the use of imprisonment, for example, is very differently applied in the US compared to some western European countries. This means that sentencing policy is also unlikely to have caused the international crime drop. Rather, the explanation lies in the fact that crime is a product of many influences, including the state of the economy, the cohesiveness of communities, and so on. Drug use, for example, is a prime cause of offending. The proliferation of drugs such as crack cocaine and heroin in the early 1980s triggered an escalation in crime and criminal violence. In fact, recent research shows clear links between the decline in crime after 1995 and the decline in drug use. Fewer drugs means less crime.

Responding to crime without going to court

In the US, low-level criminality—misdemeanours rather than the more serious felonies—is often charged by the police, causing a silting up of the lower level courts. The crimes are often trivial, unlike the consequences—offenders receiving convictions also gain an official criminal record. Other countries have attempted to reduce the caseload of the courts by resolving cases *before* they come to trial. A range of options have been created to respond to crime or disorder without involving the courts. Most of these 'out of court' disposals are imposed by the police.

The arguments in favour of these schemes are powerful. Perhaps the most widespread criticism of the courts is that they often deal with matters too trivial to justify prosecution, the individual being charged with a mere misdemeanour. Everyone who has spent some time in a criminal court will, I am sure, have at some point asked themselves questions such as, 'What is this case doing here?' And 'Why is this person being prosecuted for such a trivial crime?'. Whether from the perspective of the defendant or the State, prosecutions should be reserved for cases which simply cannot be resolved in any other way. People who have had no prior involvement in the CJS should be prime candidates for receiving alternatives to prosecution. Out of court disposals, on the other hand, are less appropriate in cases of serious crime, persistent offending, or where allegations are being contested. Although the news media highlight cases of serious crime where the police have simply issued a caution, these are very rare—only around 70 cases in the UK in 2014.

The benefits of out of court disposals are clear, but their use has attracted critics who note the potential for injustice: unlike a criminal proceeding which comes before a judge, out of court disposals do not involve lawyers. The person subject to an order must decide whether to accept the punishment imposed or be taken to court. There is a danger of injustice as 'out of court' also means 'out of sight'. Another criticism of out of court disposals comes from people who see the related incidents as being too serious to resolve without a trial. In England, a range of out of court disposals exist, including warnings for adults suspected of drug offences and fixed penalty notices for disorderly behaviour. We'll focus on two of the more common disposals to illustrate the benefits and dangers of this form of criminal justice response to crime.

'On the spot' fines

Public disorder of various kinds—such as drunkenness or vandalism—is a problem for all Western nations. The problem has become worse due to a general increase in affluence accompanied by a decline in the cost of alcohol. The court system cannot possibly process all these cases of disorder—hence the need for *penalty notices for disorder* (PNDs), as they are known in England. In the past, officers took drunks to the police station to sleep off the effects of their excessive drinking; nowadays, with growing urban populations, there are too many such individuals to accommodate in police cells. Instead, the police have resorted to imposing 'on the spot' fines for public drunkenness, as well as a range of other antisocial behaviours.

The fine is imposed immediately but the individual is given time to pay. If the fine is paid, the matter is closed. If not, the fine is increased and the matter is referred to the courts for enforcement. The individual on whom the PND is imposed is not convicted of a crime; he will not acquire a criminal record, although his name will enter the police database. This will have consequences for future contacts with the police. If there is a victim involved, the police will take into account the victim's view of the level of punishment that should be imposed. PNDs seem a reasonable response to a widespread, low-level problem. Cautions for more serious allegations of wrongdoing, however, take us into deeper waters.

Official cautions

Forty years ago, a noisy dispute between neighbours would have been resolved by a visit from the police. An officer would have recorded some details about the incident and warned the people involved. In most cases this did the trick, and peace was restored. Nowadays, police have greater powers, but their professional conduct is under greater scrutiny. As a result, verbal warnings have been replaced by the issuing of a formal caution known as a 'conditional caution' (in other words, a warning which carries conditions). Those receiving a caution must accept responsibility for the offence in question—they must plead guilty, which they usually do without first seeking legal advice. In addition they must agree to abide by the conditions imposed—if they fail to comply with the conditions, they face prosecution. The conditions imposed will be rehabilitative or reparative—promoting the improved welfare of the offender or the victim, respectively.

Cautions are not intended for cases of serious offence. If the police deem it likely that a court would respond to a given offence by ordering a tough community penalty or a term of imprisonment, then the police should charge the offender rather than issuing him with a caution. As such, in more serious cases the police will normally consult a prosecutor before issuing a caution. Conditional cautions do, however, still carry serious consequences for an offender.

For example, even once the caution's attached conditions have been successfully completed by an individual and the period of the caution has expired, the individual's name and the details of the caution they received will remain in the official databases and may emerge in job applications or any later criminal proceedings. Before closing this section, it is worth noting that visible minorities are less likely to receive an out of court disposal and more likely to be taken to court than are White offenders. This suggests differential treatment with respect to the choice of penalties.

Bailing the defendant

All jurisdictions have schemes which permit a person charged with an offence to remain in the community until their first appearance at court; this is known as 'bail'. The right to bail has been described as being as 'old as the law of England itself'. Most people are granted bail by the police; others are bailed following a court hearing. The court will normally impose a surety to ensure that the accused adheres to the conditions of release. Like most decisions involving financial penalties, the level of the surety will reflect an individual's means.

There is a presumption in the system for releasing individuals on bail. The reasons for this presumption are two-fold. First, if the accused is detained in prison it is harder for him to prepare a defence to the charge he is facing; second, if he is acquitted, detention prior to a trial would be punishment in the absence of a conviction. The CJS seeks to bail as many accused individuals as possible. The presumption of innocence requires the State to punish only those found guilty—and detention is a punishment, regardless of the reasons given for its use.

Despite the recognition that it is important to allow defendants their liberty while they await trial, remand prisoners account for a high percentage of the incarcerated population. There are approximately three million people in pre-trial detention around the world, and there are more countries with an increasing rather than declining remand population. In many African countries, over half the prisoners are awaiting trial. Remand populations tend to be much lower in western Europe, but they still account for significant numbers of prisoners.

In determining whether to detain or release an accused, a court will address several questions, including the following:

- Will the accused appear in court when required?
- Will the accused commit an offence if released on bail?
- Will the accused interfere with the course of justice—for example, by threatening a potential witness?

If a court is satisfied that there are substantial grounds for believing that the defendant will fail to appear for trial, commit an offence, or interfere with a witness, the defendant may be remanded to custody. Other considerations for a court deciding on bail will be any previous failures of the individual in question to surrender to authorities. Release may also be denied if the court believes that it is in the defendant's own interest (his safety is at risk, or he is a young person without a fixed residence).

Release on bail often carries conditions. These are imposed to ensure that the defendant appears at court and/or that he does not commit an offence while on bail. Ensuring his appearance at court may mean that he is required to report to a police station at regular intervals, and may have travel restrictions imposed or even a curfew. For example, people on bail may have to surrender their passport. In rare cases electronic monitoring may be imposed in order to ensure the bailed individual remains within a specific area. Almost all persons on bail do comply with their conditions, with the failure to do so generally resulting in committal to custody (remand detention); those committing an offence while on bail receive harsher punishment than they would have done outside of a bail situation; and, finally, almost all defendants released on bail do appear at court.

False positives and false negatives

The data on case outcomes suggest that the CJS is often too conservative in its bail decisions. A significant proportion of those denied bail due to risk of re-offending or fleeing the jurisdiction could in fact have been safely granted bail. This seems particularly likely considering that almost half of these individuals subsequently receive merely a community penalty—raising the question of why they had been detained in the first place.

There is a general criminal justice lesson here: many decisions err on the side of caution. Accused persons who do not constitute a real risk are denied bail; offenders who can be safely punished in the community are sentenced to prison; and prisoners who are unlikely to offend if released are denied parole. Such cases are known as 'false positives': the CJS predicts an outcome (re-offending) that turns out to be wrong. The opposite problem of course is 'false negatives': the CJS assumes the offender may safely be released on bail or let out of prison, and he goes on to commit a serious crime. False negatives create headlines; false positives remain unseen. There is evidence from several countries that when a high profile false negative occurs—for example, someone on bail commits a serious crime—criminal justice decision-makers become more conservative in future cases in their desire to reduce further such occurrences.

Pre-trial developments

After arrest, the prosecution guides the proceedings. The prosecutor is a little-known, poorly understood legal professional. When most people think about lawyers, defence advocates come to mind, real or fictional: Clarence Darrow, F. Lee Bailey, Allen Dershowitz, Kavanagh Q.C., or Rumpole of the Bailey. It's much harder to come up with a famous prosecutor—in fact or fiction. Most people have only a vague—often unrealistic—idea of what a prosecutor does A few years ago I conducted a survey of the general public in which I asked people what they knew about prosecutors and the prosecution branch of criminal justice. I found very low levels of knowledge; people had only a vague idea of the work of prosecutors. Most people subscribed to a number of misperceptions. For example, most respondents assumed that the prosecutor represents the victim in the same way that a defence lawyer represents the accused. Not so. The prosecutor represents the State.

Prosecutors and defence advocates share a duty as officers of the court to not mislead the court. However, prosecutors face unique professional challenges. Defence lawyers promote the best interests of their clients: a clear mandate which guides the course of the representation. The prosecutor, on the other hand, considers the interests of the State, a more complex mandate to discharge. Furthermore, a prosecutor does not single-mindedly pursue a conviction in counteraction to the defence advocate's pursuit of an acquittal. The prosecutor must weigh the wider interests of justice and this may mean refraining from prosecuting a suspect, discontinuing a prosecution, or disclosing key evidence that may lead to the exoneration of the defendant. Today, the prosecutor's role is further complicated by the need to interact with the victim—by providing information or (in some jurisdictions) consulting the victim about key decisions. A defence lawyer simply consults the client.

To charge or not to charge

In some countries, the police lay charges; elsewhere the charging decision is in the hands of the prosecution branch of criminal justice. The prosecutor's first decision is whether to prosecute a suspect by authorizing a criminal charge. The prosecutor applies a two-stage test before launching a prosecution. First, is there a reasonable prospect of conviction? And, second, is it in the public interest to prosecute?

In answering the first question the prosecutor will weigh the evidence carefully. If the case is flimsy and unlikely to result in conviction, prosecuting the defendant wastes court resources. Even if the evidence against the accused is compelling and a conviction likely, a prosecution may still not be in the public interest. There will be cases where despite overwhelming evidence supporting a conviction, a prosecution should not be launched. Consider an 80-year-old who has helped her terminally ill husband kill himself. Assisting a suicide is illegal in many countries, including the UK. The woman admits providing the assistance—she purchased the drugs and helped him swallow the pills—but she refuses to plead guilty. Most people, I suspect, would not want to see this woman on trial; they would regard it as not being in the public interest, regardless of whether the case against her was watertight.

If a criminal prosecution is launched, the prosecutor will hope that it can be resolved without a trial. At this point the defendant can prevent what may be a lengthy judicial process requiring several court appearances over many months. He can stop the criminal justice train in its tracks by pleading guilty.

Negotiating justice: 'let's make a deal'

Plea bargaining is one of the most controversial practices in criminal justice. (I prefer the term 'negotiated justice', because it is not always the case that the defendant gets a bargain. The word 'bargain' suggests someone got away with something, as in the full price for a book is £50 but you paid only £19.99; but let's stick with the more common term.)

Plea bargaining involves discussions leading to an agreement between the parties (the State, represented by the prosecution, and the accused, represented by his lawyer). For example, the accused is charged with murder, but claims he did not intend to kill or even to cause serious harm (which is the required level of intent for a murder conviction in England and Wales). After reviewing the evidence, the prosecution believe otherwise but is concerned that it may not be able to prove the murder beyond a reasonable doubt. The result may be an agreement that the accused will enter a plea to manslaughter. This plea will have to be entered in court before a judge.

This agreement may, in some countries, include a 'joint submission' on sentencing. For example, both parties may agree to recommend an eight-year prison sentence to the judge. Under these conditions the court will normally accept the recommendation. Why? First, under the adversarial model of justice, if the parties are satisfied with a particular outcome, it is unreasonable to interfere with the agreement (unless the judge believes that an injustice will result). Second, if judges routinely reject a joint submission and impose some other penalty the parties would soon cease to discuss the plea—in future discussions, the prosecution would not be able to guarantee that the State (i.e., the court) would impose the sentence 'offered' to the accused. Having said this, the courts do sometimes reject a position agreed by the two parties. A good example of this is the case of the man convicted of serial killings in Yorkshire, England. Although the parties had agreed to a plea to manslaughter, the judge rejected this and following a lengthy trial the defendant was ultimately convicted of murder.

In *theory*, plea bargaining benefits both parties. The accused benefits through receiving a more lenient sentence; the State has secured a conviction without the time and expense of conducting a trial. However, in *practice*, things are rather different. In the US in particular, defendants who plead guilty generally get little reward.

The accused has generally only one card to play: he can plead guilty. Yet it's a powerful card, which can save the State a lot of money and time. The defendant may also be able to offer some other assistance to the State—testifying against other individuals or providing information which will help prosecute other suspects. The prosecution may make concessions to incentivize the defendant to plead guilty. It may agree to: (i) reduce the number of charges against the accused (*charge* bargaining); (ii) accept a common set of facts about the case which is more advantageous to the defendant (*fact* bargaining); or (iii) accept a joint submission on the sentence (*sentence* bargaining).

Plea bargaining has many critics within and outside criminal justice. When the public are asked about plea bargaining they assume that offenders benefit greatly, but not the State. The public see it as a way for the CJS to make its job easier, even if this means going easy on defendants. For this reason, they oppose the practice. Conservative critics argue that offenders receive more lenient treatment than is deserved. Liberal critics argue that defendants are subject to excessive punishment: they claim that prosecutors lay as many charges as they can in order to build a strong hand for future negotiations with the defendant's lawyer. There is evidence that this happens in countries where plea bargaining is most active; prosecutors sometimes 'over-charge' in order to give themselves some bargaining chips in discussions with the defendant. Plea bargaining is very widespread in the US, less prominent or visible in other Western CJSs.

CJSs without *active* discussions between the parties entailed in plea bargaining still offer incentives to accused persons who plead guilty rather than contesting the charge. This policy of mitigating punishments for those who plead guilty probably explains why most defendants elect to plead guilty rather than be tried. Even in England, where discussions between the defendant and the prosecution are rare, approximately four out of five defendants plead guilty, thereby saving the State from having to prove the charge in court.

Sentence reductions for a guilty plea

Active plea bargaining may be a largely US-based phenomenon, but almost all common law systems offer sentence discounts to people who plead guilty. Why should the CJS offer rewards to defendants who plead guilty rather than insist on their day in court? The answer is that a guilty plea benefits the State in many ways. If the State does not have to run a trial there are significant cost savings. A prosecution for robbery might take many weeks of preparation, consume two to three days of court time, and cost £30,000 (US$40,000)—all of which is saved if the accused pleads guilty. Second, if the defendant pleads guilty, the prosecution is guaranteed a conviction; if a trial takes place, an acquittal may result. Third, victims and witnesses are spared the time, expense, and trouble of having to testify. Testifying creates anxiety, particularly if the case involves a sexual offence. Anyone who has been cross-examined by a clever trial advocate (most are clever) will know it can be an unpleasant experience. Finally, a system which allows the accused to enter a guilty plea offers those who are guilty a way of accepting responsibility and getting on with their lives—once the sentence has been imposed. The State should reward people who have the honesty to admit their fault without making the State prove it in a court of law. Why, in light of these arguments, would you not offer incentives to plead?

The limited time offer

The savings for the State—and the benefits for victims and witnesses—are greatest when the accused pleads at the first chance to do so. For this reason, the maximum discount is awarded when the accused enters an early plea. In England, a prompt guilty plea earns the offender a one-third discount off the sentence. If the accused waits until the day of trial, the reduction declines to a modest 10 per cent. The maximum reduction of one-third is found in many jurisdictions around the world. There seems to be a consensus that lower reductions would not affect defendants' decision-making, while greater reductions would be overly generous.

Are sentence reductions appropriate? As with active plea bargaining, opinions differ. Academics disapprove of incentives which may distort sentencing. The argument is that the offender will not get his 'just deserts': if the crime warrants six years, why impose only four? Academic lawyers also worry about encouraging wrongful convictions and express concern that the discount scheme undermines the presumption of innocence. The State should be required to prove the offence against the accused. This obligation should not be short-circuited by bribing the accused to plead guilty. Critics argue that guilty plea discounts are not so much a *discount* for those who plead guilty but rather a *penalty* for accused persons who elect to contest the charge and go to trial.

Furthermore, allowing the State to offer substantial sentencing discounts to defendants who plead rather than contest the charge can lead to wrongful convictions. I once served as an expert witness in a case involving a man charged with drug trafficking. Let's call him Tom. He pleaded guilty and freely admitted that his four previous convictions for drug crimes had been 'a fair cop'—he had indeed committed those crimes. On this occasion, however, Tom was adamant that the drugs had been planted on him by a rival dealer who had then tipped off the police. Why, then, did he decide to plead guilty? The reason was that by doing so, he received 'only' a two-year prison sentence. Had he been convicted following a trial, with his criminal record, he was looking at serving four years in prison. The discounted sentence was too good to refuse. However, if he was indeed not guilty, an injustice was done.

Modest sentence discounts seem an appropriate concession to defendants who accept responsibility for their crimes. The cost to 'doing justice' seems relatively minor and the benefits to the State and the crime victim seem striking. But the CJS should monitor the practice carefully to ensure that bargaining and sentence reductions don't get out of hand. We have heard many calls over the years for plea bargaining or sentence discounts to be abolished. Abolition is unlikely: if only about a quarter of the cases that now get resolved by plea have to proceed to trial, the courts would gum up, creating long delays in reaching a verdict. In fact, this is the norm in common law countries: most accused—about two-thirds—plead guilty. Although there is a great deal of media attention to criminal trials, the truth is that they are rare. In the US, almost all cases are resolved with a plea, usually following negotiations between the defendant's lawyer and the district attorney's office. Even in England and Wales where plea discussions are rare, 80 per cent of defendants plead guilty.

If the defendant declines to enter a guilty plea at their first appearance in court (or in a pre-trial conference or hearing), a date will be set for the parties to re-appear and argue their positions before the judge—or judge and jury.

Chapter 3
In court and on trial

Once a trial date is set, the parties prepare for the hearing in court. They will make their respective cases before an objective adjudicator. There is considerable variation in terms of the nature of the decision-making body—whether it's a judge and jury or simply a judge, for example—as well as the ways that the adjudicator is appointed.

Prosecutors and judges: elected or appointed?

In almost all countries, prosecutors and judges are appointed. They are normally senior legal practitioners with considerable experience in criminal litigation. In contrast, across the US many states elect their prosecutors and judges. Is this a good idea? The benefit of electing individuals is allegedly that elections make both professions more responsive to the community—so that they prosecute (and sentence) in ways that reflect community values. To me, the counter argument seems more compelling. If prosecutors or judges are dependent upon their popularity for professional advancement, this may distort their decision-making. They may also adopt a more 'populist' approach—prosecuting where they think the public will approve. When seeking election, prosecutors in the US often advertise their 'get tough' credentials, or cite their success rates in prosecuting offenders. This is contrary to the spirit of a prosecutor who should pursue the public interest and not simply seek a conviction in every case. The instance where politically motivated charges were laid against the Greenpeace protesters in Russia in 2013—and then dropped weeks later—is a good illustration of the dangers of having prosecutors who lack independence. The prospect of electing judges is even more alarming—they may sentence more harshly to reflect what they perceive to be the public mood. For these reasons, it is unsurprising that no other countries have followed the US example and introduced elections for prosecutors or judges.

Judges and juries

Another key distinction is whether the decision-maker is a lay person or a professional judge. In adversarial systems of justice, defendants are tried before a judge sitting alone, a judge sitting with a jury, or a panel of lay magistrates. Most jurisdictions have moved away from using lay persons as magistrates—although in England and Wales they continue to play a vital role. In fact, the magistrates' courts in England and Wales hear and decide sentence in fully 95 per cent of cases (see Box 1). Elsewhere, trial court procedure involves a trial before a judge sitting alone or trial before a judge and jury. The role of a judge, if sitting alone, is to ensure that the parties abide by the rules of procedure.

The most common arrangement consists of a trial in which the jury decides questions of *fact*—for example, which witnesses are telling the truth, and whether all the elements of the crime have been proven beyond a reasonable doubt. The judge decides matters of *law*: for example, whether certain evidence should be entered or excluded at trial. If the jury convicts the defendant, the judge then determines the sentence. The justification for the division of labour is that twelve people are more likely than a single individual to be correct in deciding a factual matter; you don't necessarily need legal training to decide which of two witnesses is telling the truth. On the other hand, jurors are not

Box 1 Lay or professional judges?

Imagine you have been charged with a criminal offence. Who would you rather be tried by, a professional judge or members of the community sitting as lay magistrates? Lay people play a role at various stages of criminal justice—as justices of the peace, deciding issues such as bail; as jurors; and in some countries as judges. In England and Wales lay persons serve as lay magistrates. They are part of the judiciary, sitting in the magistrates' courts in panels of three. They receive some basic training upon appointment and are assisted by a legally qualified advisor. Magistrates decide whether the defendant is guilty and will impose sentence. In England, lay magistrates impose about 95 per cent of all sentences; only a small percentage of cases end up in the higher courts. Advocates of lay decision-making in criminal justice cite the advantages of having community justice—lay magistrates usually come from the local area. In addition, lay people may take more time to engage with the defendant and dispense a more humane form of justice. Critics of lay magistrates say that professional judges are more efficient, and are more likely to reach an appropriate verdict and impose a fair sentence. My own experience is that magistrates have more time to hear a case and this permits them to consider a wider range of issues. In contrast, proceedings in a busy criminal court at which a single professional judge sits alone seem more formulaic. On the other hand, since all other countries have abandoned lay adjudication in favour of professional judges, this does demonstrate that the professional model is more popular. So, on balance, who would you choose to be tried by?

trained in the law of evidence to know whether a given witness's evidence is admissible or in the law of sentencing to be able to determine an appropriate sentence. So that is where the experienced judge comes in, someone who is legally qualified and has years of experience in criminal litigation.

At the conclusion of the trial the judge will provide a 'summing-up' for the benefit of the jury. This will include a summary of all the relevant law in the case as well as directions regarding the burden of proof—which is upon the prosecution—and the standard of proof, which is that the jury must be satisfied that the defendant is guilty beyond a reasonable doubt.

As we shall see later, the public are very positive about juries. In contrast, people are more ambivalent in their evaluation of judges. When asked to rate the job that judges do, the public give them high marks for being fair and for ensuring that procedures are strictly followed in court. However, community reaction to judges is more critical when it comes to determining sentence: the public around the world see judges as being out of touch with the communities they represent; and judges are heavily (and in my view, unfairly) criticized as tending to impose overly lenient sentences. Again, surveys we have conducted in the UK, Canada, and the US routinely find that most people regard judges as being too lenient towards offenders.

Trial by jury is rare. In England only about 5 per cent of cases will be decided by a jury; the remainder will be resolved in the lower courts before lay magistrates. In other common law countries, jury trials will be even rarer. Most accused plead guilty and, of those who contest trial, many will be heard by a judge alone or a panel of lay magistrates—without a jury.

Juries

Blackstone, the famous 18th-century lawyer, described the jury as the 'glory of English criminal law', but juries do have their critics. One criticism is that they are unrepresentative of the communities they are supposed to represent. This may be true, but they are still more diverse than the professional judiciary. For example, less than 5 per cent of the judiciary in England and Wales are Black or Asian. However, Black and minority ethnic groups are much better represented in juries.

A more plausible criticism of the jury involves its apparent inability to follow the evidence in a complex trial. Trials in cases of large-scale investment frauds sometimes take months, during which jurors will have to follow and understand complex forensic accounting evidence. Since a number of such prosecutions have failed, legal practitioners have called for lengthy, complex trials to be heard by a professional judge without a jury. So far these calls have fallen on deaf ears; few politicians want to undermine such a popular element of criminal justice.

From time to time the media report examples of bizarre jury behaviour. One UK case attracted a great deal of attention and negative press for juries. After hearing evidence at trial for several weeks, the jury foreman asked the judge whether they could consider matters they had read in the news media when determining whether the accused was guilty. The judge had to remind them that their verdict needed to reflect the evidence adduced at trial and nothing else. Examples like this raise questions about the competence of juries, but it is hard to know how often jurors react in this way. Jurors are sometimes accused of being ignorant of their role in the trial process (see Figure 1).

Critics of the jury also worry about the degree to which jurors follow directions from the judge. For example, if the jury accidently hear a prejudicial statement and the judge orders them to disregard it, will they actually do so? (See Figure 2.) Since juries do not give reasons for their decisions, it is hard to know the basis of their verdicts.

Another concern is that jurors who are not legal professionals might be less able to put aside prejudicial pre-trial publicity. I served as an expert witness in a murder trial in which the defendant had made an application to be tried by a judge sitting alone—without a jury, as is normally the case for murder.

1. Jurors are sometimes accused of lacking the most basic level of legal understanding.

"I don't care what the judge says, I'm not disregarding that last statement."

2. Sometimes juries can be too independent ....

The defendant had a previous conviction for manslaughter, the details of which were chillingly similar to the facts of the current charge. Details of his prior conviction had been leaked to the newspapers. So he was on trial for murder, having been previously convicted of

44

killing someone else. The defendant's lawyer believed that while a professional judge would be able to evaluate the evidence in the current case without being prejudiced by the media reports of the earlier conviction, a jury would simply infer guilt from the prior conviction for homicide. (In the end the application was denied, the jury heard the case and convicted the defendant). However, research suggests that jurors are indeed sometimes influenced by what they read or see in the newspapers (see Figure 3).

One characteristic of jury decision-making is seen as a strength by some, a weakness by others. Unlike judges, juries don't give reasons for their decisions; they convict or acquit—and then go home. Sometimes they make decisions which fly in the face of the

3. Previous convictions can unduly prejudice jurors—and sometimes judges.

evidence—usually this means acquitting a defendant despite overwhelming evidence to justify a conviction. In the US, this practice of a jury reaching a verdict at odds with the evidence is called *jury nullification*.

An example of jury nullification can be found in the trial of Clive Ponting in the United Kingdom. Ponting was a civil servant who had leaked government documents about the decision of the government to authorize the sinking of an Argentinian battleship, the *Belgrano*, during the Falklands war. (The *Belgrano* was sailing away from, not towards, the battle zone when it was sunk with the loss of 1,000 lives). Many people thought (and still do think) that the sinking was unnecessary. Ponting wanted the truth to come out and accordingly released the papers to the press. Charged with violating the Official Secrets Act, he ran a defence to the effect that his actions were in the public interest. This was ruled out, but although the jury knew this they acquitted him of the charges.

Juries also sometimes acquit because they feel the punishment for the crime would be too harsh; because they have great sympathy for the defendant; or simply because they just don't like the law. In Canada, back in the 1970s, a physician was repeatedly charged and put on trial for conducting abortions in a private clinic, a practice that was illegal under the law at that time. Yet at every trial the jury simply acquitted him; eventually the government gave up prosecuting the doctor and the Canadian parliament subsequently changed the law to legalize abortion.

Whatever we think about jury nullification, research presents a relatively positive picture. Juries appear to act thoughtfully and to treat defendants of different races in the same way. Nullification occurs very rarely. In any event, public support for the jury remains very strong around the world. Although public confidence in the police, the courts, and the prison services has declined in recent decades, there has been no such decline in public trust in the jury. One manifestation of this level of trust is the marked preference that most people have for trial by jury rather than by judge. When asked whether they would prefer to be tried by a judge or jury, the public prefer juries over judges by a significant margin. Personally, I would prefer to be tried by a judge, particularly if the case involved complex evidence.

There is little likelihood therefore that juries will be abolished or even that the right to trial by jury will be restricted. Surveys of the public routinely demonstrate widespread opposition to any proposal to restrict the right to trial by jury. When the British public was asked in 2002 what they thought of government proposals to restrict the right to trial by jury, almost three-quarters were opposed to any such reform. In the US, public support is even stronger.

Public attitudes to criminal justice issues such as the death penalty, corporal punishment, community penalties, and the like have evolved significantly over the past thirty years. In 1976, when Americans were asked to identify the prime cause of violence, 'communism' was the most popular response. Few would hold this view today. Yet despite many changes like this in public opinion, support for the jury remains as high as it was in the 1960s.

Specialized courts: making the CJS fit the offender

For centuries now the criminal trial has followed the same model for all categories of crime and criminal. This is now changing. Over the past twenty years, specialized courts have emerged which focus on one particular form of offending and adopt a different approach; we could label these courts as 'problem-solving' courts. The best known are the *drug treatment courts* (DTCs), which handle only drug offenders—although not usually in the case of the most serious drug crimes such as trafficking. The reasoning behind the use of DTCs is that it is more effective to address the cause of a crime than simply to punish the offender.

A drug court takes a radically different approach to prosecution and punishment. The defendant is required to consent to treatment in return for a less punitive outcome. He signs up to attend drug rehabilitation and to regular urine tests to ensure that he is off drugs—'clean'—for the duration of his time in the court's jurisdiction. This may be a year or more. During that period he will return to court where his drug test results will be reported to the judge. Should the offender fail more than one test, he will be transferred to a criminal court and prosecuted (and punished) in the conventional way. On the other hand, if at the end of the year he has remained drug free, he will not be punished further.

Unlike a conventional criminal court, where the judge tells the court staff to take the convicted offender down to the cells, at the last session in drug treatment courts there is a 'graduation' ceremony. The judge congratulates the offender and the atmosphere in court is celebratory rather than condemnatory. One of the appealing aspects of DTCs is the positive nature of the experience for the defendant. Let's face it, so much of criminal justice is negative, involving the expression of blame, the imposition of punishment, or the threat of future punishment. However, in the case of a drug addict, even the most severe threats or actual punishment will not solve their problem of addiction.

Research from the US (where these courts were started and where they are most common) suggests that offenders processed through DTCs are less likely to re-offend, and less likely to relapse into drug abuse. However, DTCs are generally more expensive than a conventional court. It is early days; DTCs have been operational for only about fifteen years at the time of writing; it seems likely that, as treatment programmes evolve and become more effective, this option will take over an increasing volume of the drug offender case load.

Other specialized courts exist for different profiles of offending and offender. The legal professionals working in these courts need to have specialized knowledge of the nature and causes of the crimes they process. For example, in domestic violence courts the prosecutors and judges will have specialized training in the dynamics (and treatment) of violence in the home. The sentences that are imposed are designed to prevent re-offending. A relatively new specialized court in the US deals with war veterans charged with criminal offences. Armed services personnel returning from active duty in war zones often suffer from post-traumatic stress disorder. This can trigger alcohol and substance abuse, and sometimes offending. 'Veterans' courts specialize in devising an appropriate response to this category of offender.

In Canada and Australia, specialized courts exist for Aboriginal offenders. These courts employ lawyers with close links to the Aboriginal communities. The judges in Aboriginal courts receive advice from elders about the nature of the offending, and assistance in devising sentences which are sensitive to the Aboriginal culture and community from which the offender has come. Research has shown that people involved in these 'indigenous' courts perceive them to be fairer than the mainstream courts.

Specialist courts recognize that crime is not simply a result of 'bad people' making criminal decisions. As such, the focus of the system is not simply to calibrate a sentence with a level of severity that is proportional to the seriousness of the crime. Rather, it seeks to understand *why* the crime was committed and *how* the offender can be rehabilitated to ensure it does not recur. Criminal justice is as much about problem-solving as it is about punishing, and that's the advantage that these courts have over the conventional approach.

Juvenile courts

Juveniles are subject to a separate criminal justice regime. Adults are usually defined as individuals over the age of 18. Young offenders are those under 18 but above some minimal threshold for criminal responsibility. This lower age level varies widely around the world; in many European countries a person has to be 14 years old or older before they can be charged with a criminal offence. In England and Wales a 10-year-old can be charged with a crime. One of the most notorious crimes of the last century, the murder of James Bulger, was committed by two 10-year-olds. Many scholars question whether it is reasonable to hold 10- and 11-year-olds criminally responsible. Even if children are aware that it is wrong to commit a certain act, do they really have sufficient awareness of the nature and consequences of their actions to be subject to criminal penalties? As a result, youth courts are run very differently from their adult counterparts. The general public are not allowed in and there are restrictions on the freedom of the press to report on the identity of these young defendants. The responses of the court are very different too; the options available are designed to promote rehabilitation as much as to punish.

The separate treatment of young offenders extends to punishment in the youth court. Many people believe that when it comes to sentencing, young offenders should be treated the same as adults—if they are being convicted of the same offence. In other words, 'A crime is a crime'. There is an intuitive appeal to this slogan: after all, if you have been mugged, the shock and loss of money is no different if the mugger happens to be 16 rather than 26. However, while the crime—in terms of its impact on the victim—may be the same, this analysis fails to consider the offender's level of culpability. Sentencing schemes vary widely around the world, but all criminal justice systems (CJSs) sentence juveniles less harshly than adults convicted of the same crimes. There are several reasons why we would blame young people less than adults convicted of the same crime, and therefore punish them more leniently.

First, adolescents and young adults do not have the same life experience as mature adults and this makes them less culpable. A 15-year-old can reasonably assert that he did not fully appreciate the wrongfulness of the crime, a claim that is much less convincing from a mature adult. If he was not yet a full adult, the CJS should not punish him to the same extent as it would an adult.

The second reason for treating young offenders differently is that some 'adult' penalties are particularly inappropriate for juveniles. Imprisonment is the obvious example. Depriving an adult of his liberty will have serious consequences—on his employment, for example. However, the long-term effects of a 12-month prison sentence on, say, a 15-year-old will have a very deleterious effect on his education. This will lead to longer-term damage to his prospects in adulthood than would a simple loss of employment for the same term for an adult.

The third reason for sparing young offenders imprisonment, except in the most serious cases, is that it will separate them from their families and deny them much needed emotional support at a critical time in their moral development.

Finally, being detained in a correctional facility is more painful for these young people who have not yet developed adequate psychological coping mechanisms to deal with stressful life events. This is why self-harm and suicide rates are particularly high for young prisoners. For these reasons CJSs use imprisonment only sparingly for young offenders, resorting to detention only when it is absolutely necessary. And in cases where young people are imprisoned, they are sent to separate juvenile facilities.

Sentencing options imposed on young offenders are aimed at promoting rehabilitation. In addition, a youth court devising a sentence for a young offender will usually include the offender's family in determining the appropriate course of action. One key element of an effective criminal justice response to young people is engagement with the family. The young person's family may have played a role in the juvenile's offending—by failing to support him in school or by being inappropriate role models. One view is that crime begins in the family: attitudes to rules and laws are acquired at home and in the school. A criminal justice intervention which failed to examine the young person's family circumstances would be doomed to failure.

Whether they were part of the problem or not, families can certainly play a role in the solution. For this reason, most youth justice initiatives involve the parents of the young person from the outset. A good example of such a scheme is the family group conference concept which exists in various forms in New Zealand, Australia, Canada, and other countries. Here the idea is to create a family-based solution to the problems giving rise to the offending. Conferences adopt a wider, more holistic approach to the crime, which involves the young person's family, workplace, school, or social context.

The wrong man: when criminal justice fails

Serious failures of the CJS always generate headlines. Badly designed buildings may demoralize the occupants, but architectural failures seldom make the news (unless the structure collapses and people die). Errors by criminal justice professionals can also cost lives. Recall the innocent Brazilian man shot by London police in 2005 after the subway bombings; or the two unarmed and innocent men killed by New Orleans Police after Hurricane Katrina. Wrongful death may also occur when a sentencing court imposes the death penalty on an innocent person.

Wrongful convictions attract great publicity, often because the travesty is not rectified for years. It is hard to estimate the proportion of all cases in which a *wrongful acquittal* is recorded, but researchers have studied *wrongful convictions*. Estimates vary but about 2–5 per cent of all convictions involve an individual who was not guilty, or was guilty of a less serious offence than the one he was convicted of committing. This is a small percentage, but with the high volume of prosecutions it amounts to significant numbers of wrongfully convicted people—about 7,000 felony convictions in the US alone. In light of the fact that the prosecution must prove all the elements of the offence to the high standard of 'beyond a reasonable doubt', how can these injustices occur?

Usually there is no single cause of wrongful conviction, but rather a chain of unfortunate events or professional misconduct. The most common causes of wrongful conviction include: mistaken eyewitnesses—particularly a problem when the victim and alleged perpetrator are of different ethnicities; witnesses who lie—for example, jail house informants who claim to have heard the accused confess when in reality they are lying to gain a more lenient sentence for themselves; false confessions—people sometimes confess to crimes they did not commit, sometimes in response to intense police interrogation; 'tunnel vision' by prosecutors who settle on a particular individual and then build a case against him, ignoring evidence which suggests he is not guilty; and, finally, inadequate or incompetent legal representation for the accused. There are many notorious examples of wrongful convictions, some of which resulted in the execution of the offender. An English example is the case of Timothy Evans, who was convicted of the murder of his wife and subsequently executed. The guilty party was in fact Reginald Christie, who had been living in the same house as Evans. Evans was subsequently granted a posthumous pardon (see Figure 4).

4. The arrest of Timothy Evans for a murder committed by another suspect. The look on Evans's face tells the story.

People who are wrongfully convicted are victims of criminal justice. How does the State respond to wrongful convictions? The first step for the convicted individual is to launch an appeal through the courts. Yet experience has shown that wrongful convictions can remain in place even after review by a higher court. Another route involves external agencies to which the wrongfully convicted may apply for a review of their case. In England, the *Criminal Cases Review Commission* is one such body. The more spectacular wrongful convictions—which result in a person spending years in prison for a crime they did not commit—usually trigger a Commission of Inquiry which then recommends an appropriate level of compensation to the affected individual. Finally, the wrongfully convicted can also appeal to the Executive.

Wrongful acquittals attract far less attention from the media and scholars. While no-one likes to see a guilty party walk free from court, this kind of injustice is not as troubling as someone languishing in prison for a crime he did not commit. Nevertheless, when cases involving defendants who seem obviously guilty of a serious crime result in acquittal, this is cause for concern and attracts headlines. One reason for the publicity is the realization that in most countries the offender cannot be prosecuted a second time for the same charge. A number of countries have tried to reduce the number of such cases by allowing, under certain conditions, the State to prosecute an individual again even though he has been acquitted of the charge. This occurred in 2012 in England when defendants were re-tried (and subsequently convicted) on murder charges involving the racist killing of Stephen Lawrence. Re-trying the defendant once he has been acquitted is not permitted in the US—it is known as 'double jeopardy'. The State has one, and only one, opportunity to convict the offender on a specific charge.

Most criminal charges result in a conviction being recorded against the defendant—usually because he pleads guilty to one or more of the charges. If the defendant is convicted, either following a contested trial or because he pleaded guilty, the criminal process enters another, and even more complex stage: the determination of sentence. In civil law systems the trial and sentence are decided in a single hearing. This makes little sense: the court has to decide whether the accused is guilty and at the same time what the sentence should be. It is much better to make one decision and then adjourn so that information relevant to the second decision can be gathered. This latter arrangement occurs in common law countries. Having recorded a conviction the court rises to allow the parties and other professionals to prepare sentencing reports. So we will pause now too and reconvene in Chapter 4 to discuss sentencing.

Chapter 4
Why punish...and how?

These are the oldest and most fundamental questions in criminal justice. Legal philosophers have grappled with them for centuries, without reaching agreement. For some people the answer to the first question is obvious: to make the offender suffer for his wrongful actions. But this response doesn't take us much further. We need to clarify *why* punishment is imposed, and we need to justify the penalties we impose in individual cases. Legal justifications for punishment reflect one of two schools of thought.

One perspective focuses on the crime. State punishment demonstrates to the offender (and others) that society collectively disapproves of particular conduct. The level of disapproval will be reflected in the severity of punishment imposed. This rationale for punishing is unconcerned with future offending—what counts is what the offender has done, not whether he will do it again. The key element is the seriousness of the crime: the more serious the crime, the harsher the punishment.

In contrast, the second group of justifications relates to crime prevention—to impose a sentence which will prevent crime through a variety of means. For example, imposing a stiff sentence on juveniles convicted of carrying a bladed weapon is intended to prevent knife crime through deterrence. (It is more of a hope than an expectation; such sentences seldom deter potential offenders.)

Or, ordering an offender to perform free work for the community and address the causes of his offending is designed to prevent crime through rehabilitation. Finally, incarcerating the offender prevents crime by removing him from open society. The critical element for this perspective then is not so much the seriousness of the crime, but the risk that the offender poses in terms of future crime.

At sentencing then, a judge resembles the Roman god Janus who has two faces in order to gaze in opposite directions at the same time. Sentencing also looks in two directions: *backwards*, to assess the seriousness of the harm caused and to hold the offender accountable for that harm; and *forwards* to assess the risk the offender may pose to society.

Sentencing is the most visible and the most criticized stage of the criminal justice system (CJS). Surveys around the world routinely show that the public have less confidence in the courts than the police or other elements of the system. The reason for the low confidence in courts is that most people regard judges as too lenient. Yet the perception of leniency is founded upon misinformation. In 1982, we conducted a survey of Canadians to test their knowledge of sentencing practices. We asked people to estimate the custody rate for common crimes like robbery or burglary, and found that approximately three-quarters of the sampled population under-estimated custody rates by a significant degree. Similar questions have been posed in many other countries since then, including Australia, Barbados, and the United Kingdom, with the same result. For example, in the UK in 2013, the average sentence for rape was about nine years in prison, but when we asked the public to estimate the length of imprisonment for this offence, most people provided much shorter terms. This misperception is a result of the skewed media coverage of sentences: odd, or unusually lenient, sentences attract headlines and then people assume these cases are typical of all sentences imposed.

Small wonder then that so many people feel that judges are not doing a good job sentencing offenders.

Sentencing objectives

The phrase 'doing justice' reflects the perspective which looks backward to the offence, rather than to the future. Doing justice consists of imposing a sentence which corresponds to the seriousness of the crime and the offender's blameworthiness. A court measures the seriousness of the crime against other instances of the same crime as well as other crimes. It also decides how much the offender should be blamed, and then constructs a penalty which corresponds to this calculation. This creates a proportion between the crime and the punishment—known as the principle of *proportionality* in sentencing. All common law countries apply this principle. For example, in Canada the Criminal Code states that the sentence 'must be proportionate to the harm caused and the degree to which the offender was responsible'. Similar provisions exist in many other jurisdictions such as New Zealand and Israel. This approach is sometimes described as 'making the punishment fit the crime'.

One common criticism is that sentences don't always fit the crime. This can occur in several ways. A sentence may be too harsh relative to the seriousness of the crime, or it may be too lenient relative to the harm caused to the victim. Judges are sometimes criticized for punishing property crime more harshly than crimes of violence (see Figure 5). Generally speaking, however, courts do a good job in ensuring a fit between the crime and the punishment. As we'll see later, at sentencing judges often have guidance regarding the kinds of sentences appropriate to various crimes.

Another classic sentencing objective is to prevent crime through deterring the offender—or other potential offenders. Two forms of deterrence exist: *general deterrence*, according to which penalties are imposed to deter other potential offenders; and *special*

5. Does the punishment always fit the crime?

deterrence, where the goal is to deter the individual before the court. General deterrence is more controversial as it contains the potential for injustice. Some judges assume that they can control the crime rate by 'cracking down' on offenders convicted of a particularly frequent or serious crime. They impose a much harsher sentence than can be justified by the seriousness of the crime—specifically in order to deter others. When this happens, the offender is being punished not so much for what he has done, but for what others *may* do in the future. This seems unfair, or as the philosopher Immanuel Kant put it, 'one man ought never to be dealt with as a means subservient to another'.

An example of this type of deterrence occurred in Britain in 1963: the so-called Great Train Robbery, when a gang stopped a train and made off with £2 million. The sentencing judge took the view that robbing trains was a new form of offending that had to be stopped in its tracks, so to speak. He imposed thirty-year prison terms on almost all the robbers. Thirty years is longer than the term of imprisonment served by offenders convicted of offences involving death; the sentence was much harsher than usual in order to deter other potential offenders from committing that crime.

Fifty years later, the courts in England again imposed heavy deterrent sentences—this time for crimes during the summer riots in 2012. Over a couple of days in the summer, riots took place in several cities. For example, some young people had the not-so-bright idea of placing an appeal on Facebook encouraging others to start a riot. It was meant as a not-so-funny joke. The offenders received six-year prison sentences, reduced to four years for pleading guilty. That would be a typical sentence for a far more serious crime, such as aggravated assault or manslaughter. Again, the severity of the sentence imposed was not so much to do with the seriousness of the specific crime, but rather to prevent other potential offenders.

Does deterrence actually work? We are all deterred in various contexts by the thought of punishment; we all make cost–benefit calculations. For example, George is running late for the theatre but can make the first act if he parks illegally in a nearby side street. If he does, he might be lucky and escape without a fine. Alternatively, he may return to find a £100 parking ticket on his windscreen, making it an expensive night out. Having made some quick mental calculations he decides to park legally further away, thus avoiding the possible parking fine. The threat of a punishment has deterred him.

This everyday example contains important lessons about general deterrence. First, before people can be deterred they have to consider the consequences of their actions. Unfortunately, much criminal behaviour is unplanned or committed without reflection—offenders who do not plan to commit crime cannot be deterred. For example, when many offenders commit a crime, they are inebriated, under the influence of drugs, or in a state of heightened emotion. These states of mind are hardly conducive to rational decision-making. If sentences are going to deter potential offenders, the target audience must be people who are forward-thinking, rational, and sober, and this is seldom the case.

Unfortunately, this argument is generally lost on politicians, most of whom assume that the best way to deter crime is to simply make the penalties harsher. In reality, efforts should go towards increasing the likelihood of conviction rather than the severity of sentences. This means more police and more effective prosecutors rather than longer prison sentences. Research reveals that deterrence is a poor way of preventing crime—most offenders are hard to deter, for the reasons already noted. This is a generalization, and while some crimes are particularly hard to deter, for others deterrence may have some effect. Crimes by corporations and high status white collar crimes may be deterred more effectively because offenders tend to be more rational, seeking opportunities where the payoff will be high and the potential penalty low.

Rehabilitation

Another familiar and very important sentencing objective is rehabilitation. Here the idea is to prevent crime by *reforming* rather than *threatening* the individual offender with additional punishment. The objective is controversial because some people feel it's inappropriate (or even impossible) to impose reformation: it must come from within the individual. Imagine an offender with a drinking problem which triggers his offending. Should a court *order* him to follow an alcohol abuse treatment programme or to join Alcoholics Anonymous? Probably not; he has to want to change.

Many offenders want to reform themselves. They know they require treatment or assistance, but often they need encouragement.

At sentencing, a court will carefully consider the sentencing options which might promote rehabilitation. This is an area where judges are least well qualified. Judges are well placed to make decisions about the seriousness of the crime or the offender's level of culpability, but they are not experts in knowing what a person might need to turn his life around. For this reason courts turn to probation services and other professionals who are knowledgeable about the interventions available, and which ones will benefit this specific offender. Effective sentencing involves many more professionals than just judges. Once the offender leaves the court, whether bound for prison or to serve a sentence in the community, his rehabilitation is in the hands of the people who administer the sentence. In this respect the court is creating the conditions which seem most propitious in terms of helping the offender. Probation officers, parole supervisors, State and voluntary agencies all play a role in administering the sentence.

The most common question in the field of rehabilitation is, 'What works?'. Our knowledge of rehabilitation has increased dramatically as a result of research over the past thirty years. Yet, there is still no 'silver bullet'; criminal behaviour is too complicated, the product of too many forces. A rounded approach is necessary, one which identifies the offender's needs, and reduces his risk factors. Some of these risk factors and needs are obvious, others less so. Penal interventions which address barriers to employment and stable accommodation have proved successful in turning offenders' lives around. Desistance from crime is a slow process, and although many offenders attempt to desist, they often fail and need additional opportunities and encouragement—the sentence meted out by the court can assist in this respect.

Sentencing objectives in practice

The number of different and potentially conflicting sentencing objectives creates a problem: How do courts decide which objective is appropriate in any given case? Left to their own devices, judges may head in different directions in response to the same case. One may feel that the offender can be rehabilitated, and impose a community penalty, while another might believe that the crime is so serious that only imprisonment is appropriate, meaning that rehabilitation will take a back seat. Analyses of sentencing judgments and experiments with judges in the 1970s and 1980s confirmed this kind of disparity. Judges tended to have pet theories about what worked and which objectives were appropriate in which cases; some would favour rehabilitation, some punishment. Lawyers were not slow to spot this, and in some countries lawyers would manoeuvre arrangements to ensure that their case got before a judge who was most likely to order the verdict they were seeking. This still happens, and is known as 'judge shopping'.

Most countries have passed a law which specifies the sentencing objectives that their courts should follow. The hope is that if courts are all working towards the same set of objectives, consistency will result, but it is more a hope than an expectation. Simply listing the objectives without providing any guidance on how to reach those objectives in the various possible circumstances is unlikely to result in consistency. It's a bit like giving diners an extensive menu of dishes and still expecting them all to choose the same entrée.

What more information—beyond the sentencing objectives—would a court need in order to sentence offenders in a consistent way? Quite a lot, actually: legal principles to follow at sentencing; knowledge of the sentences imposed on offenders convicted of similar crimes in the past (legal precedents); recommendations from the offender's lawyer; guidance from the prosecutor on the State's views about the appropriate sentence; a report on the offender's background, family, and employment situation from the probation service; the victim's statement about the impact of the crime (see Chapter 6). This is just some of the information that a judge will consider before imposing sentence. In addition, where there are sentencing guidelines, the judge would need to consider those guidelines also before making a decision.

There are two essential features of sentencing in common law countries. First, there is considerable discretion for courts. Second, there is a wide range of sentencing options available to courts. The consequence is a fair degree of variability in sentencing outcomes. Recognition of the existence of disparity has led several countries to adopt sentencing guidelines which restrict judicial discretion and make sentencing more predictable and consistent.

Sentencing disparity

How much difference does the judge personally make to the sentence imposed? Ideally, given the same case, all judges would impose the same sentence, the way that a student's essay should receive the same grade—whichever faculty member happened to be marking the work. Unfortunately, as offenders (and students) will attest, judges (and professors) differ in their perceptions of the same criminal case (or essay). Variation in sentencing has been demonstrated repeatedly by researchers over the past century, using a variety of research methodologies. Sometimes they study actual sentencing trends—and find that sentences vary on the court location.

Sentencing disparity has been demonstrated in many ways in different countries. Researchers have given groups of judges the same case to read and then asked them to sentence the offender. If the personality of the judge is unimportant, the sentences should vary little. Yet the studies that have adopted this experimental approach have found considerable variation. One study asked 200 judges to pass sentence on the same case of armed robbery. The least severe sentence chosen was a suspended prison sentence, while the most severe was thirteen years in prison! The range in response to another case—of theft this time—ran from a fine to three years in prison. These findings have been replicated in other countries and on different occasions; they underline the need for some form of guidelines which would promote a uniform approach to sentencing across courts and judges.

The sentence of the court

Under the adversarial model of criminal justice, both prosecution and defence will normally propose a specific sentence, and they will support the proposal with arguments and prior sentencing decisions. At the sentencing hearing, the prosecution will highlight important aggravating factors and may summarize or read portions of the *victim impact statement*. The defence advocate will prepare a submission in mitigation, again supported by precedents. In most (but not all) countries the sentencing judge will therefore have balanced (and detailed) recommendations to consider. Preparing these sentencing submissions can take time—which is another reason for delaying sentencing. In addition, probation services often prepare a 'pre-sentence' report on the offender to assist the court. This report will discuss any problems he is experiencing and will help the court decide which kind of sentence to impose. For example, the report may note that despite having committed a relatively serious crime, the offender has a supportive family and is gainfully employed with a good work record going back several years. Knowing this may encourage a court to spare the offender imprisonment, and suspend the prison sentence.

The nature and severity of any sentence is determined by the seriousness of the offence (*harm*) and the extent to which the offender should be blamed for the offence (*culpability*).

Seriousness is reflected in the harm caused or risked. Actual harm is relatively straightforward to measure: how much damage was done or property stolen? How many victims were there and how extensive were their injuries? Information on these matters will emerge from testimony at trial. In the event of there being no trial (because the accused pleaded guilty), the prosecutor will draw upon the victim impact statement to help establish the full seriousness of the offence.

Culpability is a more complicated concept to define and measure. The key question is: how much is the offender to blame for the crime? For many crimes, although the offender's actions were illegal, there can be reasons why he may be less to blame. Imagine an offender convicted of assault—punching another person in the face. If prior to the assault the victim had racially abused the offender, this reduces the latter's culpability. He will still be convicted of assault: being called a racist name does not *excuse* the crime, but it will *mitigate* the punishment imposed. If the assault was spontaneous and totally unprovoked, then the offender is fully culpable and there will be no such mitigation. First-time offenders, juvenile offenders, and so on are generally regarded as being less culpable. People who carefully plan a crime and wilfully ignore warnings that the act is criminal are judged to be more culpable.

Guidance for courts at sentencing

In addition to specifying the objectives of sentencing most countries assist courts in deciding on sentencing by creating laws which specify important mitigating and aggravating factors—such as whether the accused pleaded guilty, expressed remorse, or has prior convictions; and the key sentencing principles—for instance that imprisonment should only be imposed if no other sanction is sufficient to the purpose, or that the severity of the sentence should reflect the seriousness of the offence. But this guidance is relatively light-touch; these laws do not prescribe specific sentences for particular crimes. Courts need more guidance, and for this reason a number of countries do provide clearer guidelines.

Sentencing guidelines contain a range of sentences suitable for each offence and courts are encouraged to impose a sentence within that range. The oldest and best-known sentencing guidelines exist across the US. For example, in the state of Minnesota, a Commission administers the guidelines which are presented in a grid (see Figure 6).

This sentencing grid is modelled in the same way as, for example, mileage charts, where departure cities are listed along one axis and the destinations along the other. A judge can locate the appropriate row for the seriousness of the crime. If the offence is a very serious assault (first degree), this would be a row 9 offence. Then the judge would look up the offender's criminal record: say, he has several prior convictions and so has a criminal history score of 4. Looking along row 9 to column 4, the judge can see that the prescribed guideline range is 114–160 months. This means that the judge must impose a sentence between these limits. In this system, judges have the authority to go below or above this range, but they must give reasons for so doing. In practice, most sentences in Minnesota fall within the guidelines' ranges.

Critics say that this grid system is too simplistic and overly rigid; that it reduces a complex and human decision to something that is rather mechanical. They also argue that it is hard, within such a system, to accommodate the wide range of relevant aggravating and mitigating factors. In favour of the grid system we can say that everyone knows where they stand. The sentence that will be imposed is much clearer under this system compared to the traditional model where a judge weighs the submissions and then selects a sentence (or combination of sentences) from a range of options.

The US grid system has not been adopted anywhere else, although a different guideline model has been implemented in England and Wales. English courts apply a separate guideline for each offence and follow a step-by-step approach to determining the sentence. This helps to promote a consistent approach to sentencing across the country. Other common law

CRIMINAL HISTORY SCORE

SEVERITY LEVEL OF CONVICTION OFFENSE (Example offenses listed in italics)		0	1	2	3	4	5	6 or more
Murder, 2nd Degree (intentional murder, drive-by-shootings)	11	306 261-367	326 278-391	346 295-415	366 312-439	386 329-463	406 346-480	426 363-480
Murder, 3rd Degree Murder, 2nd Degree (unintentional murder)	10	150 128-180	165 141-198	180 153-216	195 166-234	210 179-252	225 192-270	240 204-288
Assault, 1st Degree Controlled Substance Crime, 1st Degree	9	86 74-103	98 84-117	110 94-132	122 104-146	134 114-160	146 125-175	158 135-189

6. The sentencing grid in Minnesota: what you see is generally what you get.

countries like India and South Africa do not provide guidelines for courts. In these jurisdictions, regulating sentencing is left to the appeal courts. The idea is that if a sentence is too lenient or too harsh, the aggrieved party can appeal to a higher court. Consistency will be achieved through the higher courts regulating the trial courts, rather than by means of judges being required to follow published guidelines. Research suggests that without guidelines, sentencing decisions are less consistent. The other benefit of guidelines is that the public tend to be less critical of sentencing when they learn that courts are required to follow guidelines—rather than just imposing sentences that reflect the views of individual judges.

Mitigating and aggravating factors at sentencing

The determination of a sentence may be regarded as a weighing of all relevant mitigating and aggravating circumstances. The important word here is 'relevant'. Before a court takes a factor into account it needs to be satisfied that this factor is relevant to the sentencing decision. Factors unrelated to sentencing—such as the offender's income or social class—should be ignored. It may sound straightforward, but it is not always easy to determine whether a given factor is relevant to sentencing and, if so, how much weight it should be given.

How do we establish that a factor is relevant? One definition is that a factor is relevant if it relates to the objectives of sentencing, in other words, rehabilitation, deterrence, and punishment. For example, an offender's expressed intention to take part in a drug treatment programme is relevant to the rehabilitation purpose of sentencing. Accordingly, a court may take this fact into account and mitigate the sentence imposed.

Mitigating and aggravating factors are often taken for granted by members of the public—we all have intuitions about whether a given factor should result in a more lenient or a harsher sentence.

But many problematic circumstances exist. Factors may be considered relevant by some, irrelevant by others. Should the fact that the offender was drunk at the time of the offence *mitigate* the sentence on the grounds that the offence was uncharacteristic ('I have never acted like that before—it must have been the booze!')? On this line of reasoning intoxication sustains a more general claim by the offender that the offence was 'out of character'. Certainly, some law-abiding people commit criminal acts when they have been disinhibited by alcohol. Yet there is a counter-argument in cases in which the offender has a history of heavy drinking: he may be seen as being more blameworthy for failing to exercise some restraint regarding a known problem. On this analysis, intoxication *aggravates* the sentence. As with some other factors then, intoxication may aggravate or mitigate, depending upon the particular circumstances of the offender. Intuition alone is often a poor guide to principled sentencing.

A defence lawyer's speech in mitigation will lay heavy emphasis on personal mitigation—factors and circumstances which might convince the court to impose a more lenient sentence. These factors include: difficult family circumstances or personal loss, such as a recent divorce or the death of a close relative; extreme financial pressures, such as loss of his job; a deprived or exceptionally difficult upbringing; or that he has taken steps to address the causes of his offending. In addition, if the offender is very remorseful this is possibly the most powerful mitigating factor. Personal mitigation plays an important role in tipping the balance away from the imposition of a term of custody. A recent study found that in approximately one-third of the cases observed, personal mitigation changed what would have otherwise been a custodial sentence to a community-based sanction. So it pays to prepare a good speech in mitigation.

Although the 'top of the head' reaction of many people to crime and offenders is rather punitive, members of the public appear well aware of the importance of personal mitigation, and of recognizing the need to consider the circumstances of individual defendants. In one recent study we gave a representative sample of the public a list of factors and asked them whether they thought these should affect sentencing. The factors included items such as 'the offender was being treated for depression at the time of the offence' or 'the offender shows remorse'. We found that most people took the view that such circumstances could well justify the imposition of a more lenient sentence. For example, over three-quarters of the public believed that the expression of remorse should result in a more lenient sentence.

Principal sentencing options

What kinds of sentences do courts consider? The alternatives available to a court vary greatly from country to country, although a number are common to most. In all countries, imprisonment is the most familiar sentencing option, but is far less commonly used than a fine or a community order.

Custody can take one of several forms. A term of imprisonment can be served continuously (full-time), part-time, it can be suspended by the court, or it can be served at home. Most countries sometimes allow a person to serve the prison sentence on the weekends—*intermittent custody*. This permits him to work and support his family. He enters the prison after work on Friday and returns home Sunday night. It works well for certain offenders, principally those who are currently working and who would lose their jobs if sent to prison for several months.

If the prison term is *suspended* the offender may never actually go to prison, if he completes the specified period of time without incident. Suspended prison sentences work well for offenders who need a 'Sword of Damocles' hanging over their heads—a threat of being committed to custody if they do not obey the order. Young offenders and first offenders are examples of such people; the mere threat of punishment is often sufficient—they don't actually need to be sent to prison to 'learn their lesson'.

Recognition of the limits of imprisonment as a sanction to change offenders' lives has led many countries to try to recreate custody in the community. These *community custody* sentences permit the offender to live at home but under conditions which mirror the restrictions of prison. For example, he may have a 9 pm curfew, or may not be allowed to leave his house at all, except for authorized purposes such as going to work or attending a religious service or medical appointment. Failure to comply with these conditions results in the offender being committed to serve the balance of the sentence in prison.

International variation in imprisonment rates

Crime rates vary a great deal from one society to another, which is hardly surprising. More surprising is the variation in the judicial response to crime. The same criminal act can provoke a very different sentence, depending on the country in which the offender is convicted. Even within the developed world, the use of custody varies greatly. Comparisons are complicated by differences in the systems of justice but it is clear that the US uses prison more often than many countries. Compare the US to Holland and Germany. In the latter two European countries, imprisonment accounts for about 7 per cent of all sentences imposed. In the US, about 70 per cent of sentences involve custody. In fact, with less than 5 per cent of the world's population, the US has about one-quarter of the world's prisoners.

How do the Dutch and the Deutsch get away with much lower rates of imprisonment? Is it because crime is rare in Europe? No—the crime rates are about the same—although there are higher rates of gun crimes and homicides in the US. The answer appears to be a more punitive public reaction to offenders in the US, which then results in tougher sentencing policies. Thus there are more mandatory sentencing laws, severe sentencing enhancements for previous convictions, and other policies which result in more offenders being sent to prison, and for longer periods of time than is the case in Europe, particularly western Europe. The fact that judges and prosecutors are elected (rather than appointed) in the US may also explain the greater use of custody. Running for judicial office may encourage judges to affirm their intention to 'get tough'—which they presume will go down well with the electors.

Financial penalties

The most common sentence in all Western nations is a fine. In most countries the level of the fine is tailored to offenders' income; wealthy individuals pay a higher fine. For example, an offender might be ordered to pay a fine which represents 50 per cent of his weekly income. Indigent offenders are required to perform unpaid work in lieu of paying a fine. Determining the appropriate fine can be challenging, and a court needs to get it right: a fine that can't be paid won't be paid. Some countries consider the offender's means through the imposition of 'day fine' units. The court determines how much the offender earns per day, and then fines him an appropriate number of days. The offender is given a limited period of time in which to pay.

Fines can be used for unemployed offenders too; their State benefits such as welfare or unemployment insurance can be docked. Again, a court will have to be careful to ensure that the amount deducted does not create excessive hardship for the offender or the offender's family. If he refuses to pay, the next step may be prison, but the days when thousands of people languished in prison for failing to pay a fine are long gone. Fines benefit the State since they generate income (to the tune of about £300 million a year in England and Wales), unlike custody, which drains the public purse. Fines are also flexible and can be tailored both to the seriousness of the crime and to the individual circumstances of the offender. The downside to fines is that they are not always paid in full, and can take some time (and considerable effort) to collect.

Community-based punishments

Community-based punishments, like imprisonment, have evolved significantly over the years. Originally they involved terms of probation—the offender had to comply with some fairly minimal conditions (such as reporting periodically to a probation officer) and that was it. Then probation orders became more intense, and the number (and diversity) of conditions increased. All the while the objective was to rehabilitate the offender, and the conditions imposed were crafted to promote his reform. For example, he might be required to maintain employment, and avoid frequenting establishments where alcohol is sold.

In recent years, community-based sentences have become more punitive. Indeed the term 'community punishment' reflects this transformation. Nowadays the community order is constructed to both reform *and* punish. The most recent manifestation of this transformation can be seen in England and Wales, where a law introduced in 2013 requires community orders to contain at least one condition which is there purely as punishment of the offender. The shift towards tougher community punishments reflects several recent trends. First, many countries have encouraged courts to use these disposals instead of prison—to save money. Courts have been slow to shift from custody to community, and one explanation was that community orders were not tough enough to plausibly replace imprisonment. It is hard to come up with a community-based punishment that is as unpleasant as, say, a year in prison. Public perceptions play a role here too. One source of public opposition to the use of community punishments is that they are a 'let off', a lenient response to crime. Making these punishments tougher, it was argued, would promote public confidence in the concept and result in more widespread use of community orders instead of prison.

A court can impose any of a number of conditions, including: unpaid work—performed under supervision; activity requirements—e.g., attending a skills training seminar; prohibited activity requirement—e.g., no alcohol is allowed or no attending football matches; a curfew—e.g., the person must remain at home between the hours of 7 pm and 7 am; or a residence requirement—he must reside at a specific location and only that location. The challenge to a court is to construct a community order composed of a package of requirements that address the offender's needs and in a way that also constitutes a significant punishment. If the combination is too light, there will be insufficient punishment; if the conditions imposed are too onerous, the offender may be doomed to failure and will be returned to court for breaching conditions. In some cases, breaching the conditions of the community penalty will result in the offender being sent to prison. When this happens the offender is in some sense being imprisoned for a crime which was not serious enough to warrant custody—or he would have been imprisoned from the outset.

For the more serious cases, a court can order the offender to be subject to electronic monitoring. This involves him wearing a tracking device, usually around his ankle where it can be hidden by clothing (see Figure 7). If the offender wanders away from court-authorized locations, the monitoring device will alert the authorities. These monitoring devices are uncomfortable and can be demeaning to offenders, but they do permit them to live in the community rather than be imprisoned. Electronic monitoring should only be used when the offender represents such a high level of risk that the CJS need to know where they are at any given time. The misuse of this technology arises when a court orders the offender to wear a monitoring device when it is not absolutely necessary.

Recent years have seen an increase in the use of community-based sentences around the world. They are much cheaper than prison (about one-third of the cost) and associated with better success

7. An electronic monitor. Best to wear a pair of jeans that cover the ankle.

rates. Community orders are flexible penalties by which the offender is served with an order covering a period of time—say eighteen months. The order carries a range of possible conditions that the offender must obey. The conditions are carefully crafted to reflect the individual needs of the specific offender—so they vary from case to case. The great advantage of community-based penalties over imprisonment is that, if properly constructed, they can punish *and* rehabilitate. If the offender is ordered to compensate the victim then working in the community will help him make this compensation; in this respect the community order also helps the crime victim. Prison in contrast is an effective punishment but a very ineffective means of rehabilitation. And if the offender is either minded to make amends to his victim or ordered to do so by the court, this is unlikely to occur if he is locked up in prison.

Supervising offenders in the community

With all these people serving sentences in the community, supervision becomes a major challenge for the CJS. This is where probation and parole officers are invaluable. These professionals are the foot-soldiers of criminal justice. They lack the visibility of uniformed police, the status of judges, or the media profile of lawyers, yet their work is vital. Probation officers supervise and assist offenders who are serving sentence in the community; parole officers perform the same role for prisoners released on parole.

Originally, probation officers were social workers with specialized training in the circumstances giving rise to offending and re-offending. Their somewhat impossible mission was to achieve a balance between helping the offender fulfil his court-imposed conditions and acting in a policing capacity. If the offender violated his conditions the probation officers could decide whether to report the breach of the order or not, depending on the nature of the breach and the officer's attitude to the client. Probation officers placed heavy emphasis on engagement with the offender and his family. House calls were common and discretion was paramount.

Today, probation and parole supervision has changed. Discretion has been curtailed by protocols which mandate that the probation officer *must* report breaches to the courts. In the past the probation officer had the discretion to turn a blind eye to the occasional lapse—the client who slept through an appointment or who was found in a pub when he had been ordered to avoid such dens of iniquity. Now, if the offender breaches a condition of parole, he is returned to court for a breach hearing. Parolees who breach without lawful excuse will be recalled to prison. The changes to probation were triggered by a growing concern among politicians with risk reduction. Probation officers have moved from promoting rehabilitation to managing risk.

As well, in many countries probation officers also have to engage with crime victims. The shift has not gone down well with probation professionals.

In addition to the shift to a focus on risk management, privatization has reared its head in the field of probation too. Probation is moving into the private sector. One manifestation of this is the so-called 'payment by results' (PBR) initiative in the United Kingdom. Here the idea is to award contracts to the organizations who can demonstrate the greatest reductions in re-offending. Advocates of PBR argue that this will lead to more effective and cost-efficient supervision of offenders. I doubt it. There are obvious conflicts of interest. First, this approach seeks to minimize re-offending at all costs. Second, it encourages a competitive approach to the enterprise. Contracts will go to the most successful teams. That strategy may work with commercial franchises but not with supervising individuals. There will also be little incentive to share information and experience across teams and agencies.

Breach of the conditions can be a problem. What happens when the offender fails to complete the assigned hours of unpaid work, or stops attending a treatment programme? The usual response is to bring him back to court to explain why he has failed to comply with the order. If he refuses to resume the work or treatment, the court may send him to prison. In many countries, breaching a community order without a lawful excuse is a criminal offence for which the offender may be imprisoned. This is the last resort of course; the goal is to get the offender to complete the community penalty, not to send him to prison.

Community or custody: which is more effective?

This question assumes we can agree on the measure of success. For some people, re-offending rates are the critical issue. Others may take the view that punishment of the offender is more important than whether he re-offends. There is also an 'apples and oranges' problem. If we compare re-offending rates of people sent to prison with people given a fine or a community penalty, are we not comparing different kinds of offences and offenders? The individuals sent to prison were presumably more likely to re-offend than the group fined—it is one reason why they were sent to prison. Finally, we might need to control for the relative costs of prison, fines, and community orders. Even if one is more effective at reducing re-offending—is it more *cost effective*?

Yet it is possible to draw some general conclusions about the relative effectiveness of different sanctions. Researchers have conducted sophisticated studies which control for pre-existing offender risk levels and other confounding factors and isolate the effect that the sentence had on the subsequent re-offending rate. Offenders sentenced to prison are *more*—not less—likely to be reconvicted than comparable offenders who had been sentenced to a community-based sentence. One explanation for this paradoxical effect (the harsher sentence has a higher re-offending rate) is that prison disrupts an individual's lifestyle, employment prospects, and family life—and these are risk factors for reconviction. The result is that any deterrent effect of imprisonment is offset by the criminogenic impact of a term of custody. Prisoners serving time in prison do so surrounded by other offenders—an experience which may encourage the newer prisoners to adopt even more antisocial ways. These findings have led many researchers and scholars to call for the abolition of short prison sentences (e.g., those for periods of six months or less) and their replacement with community penalties.

You be the judge

Now that you know the essential elements of sentencing, have a crack at determining sentence in an actual case. The defendant (whom I shall call 'Mrs English') was the mother of a young man (Thomas) who had been severely disabled in an accident. He was in a coma in hospital when his distraught mother tried to end his life. Nurses prevented her, the police were called, and Mrs English was subsequently charged with attempted murder. While awaiting trial, she returned to the hospital, locked herself in her son's hospital room, and this time succeeded in killing him. She was convicted of murder, which in England and Wales (and almost every other country without capital punishment) carries a mandatory sentence of imprisonment for life. The sentence imposed by the trial judge was appealed and subsequently reviewed by the Court of Appeal. When you have decided on a sentence, turn to the Appendix to read the judgment, and to see whether you agree with the sentence imposed by the Court of Appeal.

Chapter 5
In and out of prison

The use of the prison has evolved considerably over the centuries. In the late Middle Ages imprisonment was just a way of ensuring that the offender paid a fine—he left prison as soon as he had paid the fine. Today, we seldom imprison people for failure to pay a fine; prisons are all about punishment and rehabilitation, but particularly punishment.

A term of custody is seen as an 'equal impact' punishment in the sense that a year of one person's life is the same as a year of another's (unless the offender is very elderly, with a short life expectancy). In contrast, when imposing fines, the criminal justice system (CJS) has to undertake complex calculations in terms of the offender's income and assets—a £10,000 (US$15,000) fine, for example, could ruin a low income individual yet have little or no impact on the wealthy. Imprisonment is also a flexible sanction which can be tailored to the crime: the more serious the crime, the longer the time imposed in prison. The difficulty with this form of punishment arises because society wants prison to be about more than mere punishment. We expect our prisons to punish *and* to rehabilitate. We want prisoners to emerge from prison better people—'less likely to commit more crimes'. This is easier said than done.

The state of prisons today

In the 18th century, a social reformer called John Howard rode around England and continental Europe visiting prisons. He then wrote a book on the state of European penal institutions. Howard was appalled at the conditions he witnessed and much-needed prison reforms resulted. He described one of the better English prisons this way:

> The cell was eight feet by eight feet, filthy and with the straw worn to dust and swarming with vermin. There was no accessible water and the offenders were in irons. To add to the loathsomeness of their confinement a sewer in one of the passages often made them very offensive.

Well, we have dispensed with the leg irons, and prison conditions are much improved. Nevertheless, a modern-day John Howard would find some contemporary prisons to be no less shocking. He would particularly be struck by the large numbers of prisons and prisoners—it's a growth industry. As of 2014, it is estimated that approximately eleven million people are in prison worldwide.

Prison conditions vary widely between countries. Prisons in Scandinavian countries (particularly Sweden) and Canada are relatively modern and provide the most successful rehabilitation programmes. Prison systems which invest the most resources have the greatest success in preventing re-offending. Most US prisons do little but warehouse their prisoners, increasingly in huge 'Supermax' institutions. Correctional facilities in some African and South American countries are over-crowded, dangerous, unhygienic warehouses where violent inmates interact freely with non-violent offenders.

The pains of imprisonment are well-known—having to share a small cell with other prisoners who may be dangerous or suffer from mental health problems; being confined indoors with limited

8. A typical US prison cell. Imagine being locked in here for twenty-three hours every day.

recreational opportunities; being denied sexual companionship; having visits from friends or family restricted and monitored (see Figure 8).

Prisons impose many less obvious hardships. They have high rates of assault, homicide, and accidental death by drug overdose. The public find it hard to understand how drugs and weapons get into prison. After all, aren't there endless security checks and searches? The truth is that no prison in the world has ever managed to keep drugs out; they are brought in by visitors, thrown over the walls, sent in the mail, sold by corrupt prison guards, and manufactured by the inmates. And there is a busy cottage industry in prison which creates lethal weapons out of everyday items, even something as innocuous as a toothbrush.

The threats to prisoners' health and life are not all external. The stress associated with incarceration, particularly for young offenders imprisoned for the first time, can trigger self-harm. Rates of suicide and attempted suicide in prison are much higher than those associated with similar individuals in open society. In the general population, young, working-class males have one of the lowest suicide rates. In prison, the opposite is true. English prisons are better than those in many parts of the world, yet suicide remains an important cause of inmate death and hospitalization. In 2014, almost a hundred prisoners killed themselves in English prisons. Many of these deaths were triggered by the incarceration experience. Inadequate staffing, over-crowding, inadequate mental health services, and rampant drug use contributed to these tragic deaths. Prisoners are sometimes put into solitary confinement, often for weeks or months. Usually this occurs as a punishment for violating institutional rules. It is a severe punishment. Isolation has particularly negative effects on prisoners—particularly those suffering from psychiatric disorders. Solitary confinement increases still further the risk of suicide and self-harm, yet it continues to be used as a punishment, even in the more progressive correctional systems.

Finally, the adverse consequences of serving time don't end on release from custody. Imprisonment has a long-term financial impact: ex-prisoners' employment prospects and lifetime earnings are significantly diminished. These unintended consequences of custody have later effects for other adverse life events such as divorce or family breakdown. In this sense the 'pains of imprisonment' last and last. Once a fine is paid, the consequences of the fine are over. A term of imprisonment does not end so easily. Oscar Wilde was right when he wrote that all prison sentences were sentences of death—something is permanently lost when an individual is incarcerated.

If prison fails to rehabilitate its prisoners—and cannot deter them from re-offending—re-admission rates will be high. This in turn will lead to over-crowding and over-stretched resources, which in turn make it harder for prison staff to do anything to improve prisoners' lives and prospects. It's a vicious penal circle.

Who's in prison?

Almost all prisoners (94 per cent in the US) are male. Most are convicted offenders, but in many countries—particularly Africa and South Asia—about half of all prisoners are just awaiting trial. In Western countries visible minorities of various kinds are heavily over-represented in prison populations. Blacks and Asians are over-represented in the English prison population, relative to their numbers in the general population. However, this trend is much more striking in the US: African-Americans account for about one in ten of the general population but almost 40 per cent of the prison population. In societies that were built on waves of conquest by Europeans, the indigenous populations are also over-represented in prison: Aboriginal peoples in Canada and Australia; Maoris in New Zealand. The third distinguishing characteristic of prison populations is their social class—with *lower* socioeconomic classes being most heavily represented. In short, prison is for males, racial or ethnic minorities, and the lower socioeconomic classes.

Most prisoners are unemployed when admitted to prison and many have substance abuse problems. Many suffer from a medical or psychiatric condition or disability which may have played a role in the crime, and which will make it harder for prison authorities to address the causes of offending. The proportion of prisoners with problematic backgrounds is high: around one-third have experienced or witnessed emotional, sexual, or physical abuse in the home as a child; approximately the same proportion report having family members who have a criminal record and/or a drinking problem; and almost as many inmates report having been suspended or expelled from school. About one-quarter are admitted to prison suffering from a psychological disorder such as anxiety or depression. Perhaps the most important statistic is that almost four prisoners in ten acknowledge having a family member who had served time in an adult or juvenile prison.

Women and children in prison

Women account for a small percentage of all convicted offenders and an even smaller proportion of the prison population—around 5 per cent in most countries. Historically, this has meant that female prisoners tend to serve time under harsher conditions than men. For some systems of criminal justice, female prisoners were regarded as 'too few to count'. Women were more likely to be housed in a single, large prison, which meant they were further from their families, while male prisoners were dispersed across many prisons, permitting most to be closer to home. In addition, compared to male prisoners, women in custody typically reported higher rates of distress, anxiety, and greater concern about intrusive searches. Female rates of self-harming are more than twice as high as those of males. As primary caregivers female prisoners generally suffer more from separation from their children.

Today, conditions have improved, with prison authorities in most Western nations developing more appropriate prison regimes for women. A particular focus of attention has been in ensuring that mother–child relationships are disrupted as little as possible by the former's incarceration. In England, around a quarter of a million children have a parent in prison—which can't be good for the children's education and development. Not only does parental imprisonment impair their children's life opportunities, it makes the children at higher risk for offending themselves. The sins of the father are thus visited upon, and transmitted to, the son.

We don't usually associate imprisonment with childhood, yet significant numbers of children around the world are held in correctional facilities. Even in England and Wales, which has a (relatively) well-resourced social services structure, about 3,000 children between the ages of 10 and 17 are in prison serving a sentence or awaiting trial. Most of those awaiting trial will be convicted of offences that typically will result in a community sentence: they have been detained largely because they were repeat offenders. Unsurprisingly, most of the children in custody have come from broken homes. According to one recent study, three-quarters of the imprisoned children grew up without a father. The experience of custody will make these children worse, not better. Early intervention in the lives of troubled and troublesome children is a double-edged sword. On the one hand, signs of trouble such as antisocial behaviour and truancy cannot be ignored. On the other hand, criminal justice interventions like arrest and detention can contribute to their delinquency in adolescence.

'Lifers'

Life prisoners are the fastest growing category of prisoner. There are over 140,000 life sentence prisoners in the US—about 10 per cent of the total prison population. Almost all CJSs impose a mandatory life sentence on offenders convicted of murder. In practice, most of these offenders will serve a lengthy period in prison (20–25 years is typical) and then, after release, they remain on parole for the rest of their lives. They will be subject to conditions of parole and may be recalled to prison at any point if they violate their conditions. The life sentence creates some absurd outcomes: a lifer may be recalled to prison after having served fifteen years in the community on parole without incident. The recall may be based on violation of a technical rule rather than an allegation of a fresh crime. This is why many criminologists argue that after a lifer has completed a number of years in the community without problems, the sentence should end.

Some prisoners will never leave prison alive. These have been convicted of the most serious crime (murder) and sentenced to *life without parole* (LWOP), as it is known in the United States, or, in England, a *whole life order*. The number of such natural life prisoners has grown enormously across the US as states have substituted LWOP for the death penalty. Opponents of the death penalty have long advocated the abolition of capital punishment in favour of the more humane alternative of LWOP. Yet is it more humane? LWOP may not end the offender's life, but certainly terminates life as we know it in open society.

Consider a man sentenced to LWOP and admitted to prison aged 20 (most offenders convicted of murder are in their early twenties). According to today's longevity projections, barring accidents, this person has a life expectancy of almost ninety years. Which means a prisoner could be confined for seventy or so years to a tiny cell—a mind-boggling prospect. Equally astounding is the cost. Incarcerating an offender for seventy years would cost the US taxpayer over US$4 million.

US jurisdictions are beginning to have second thoughts about LWOP. Texas and Colorado, for example, have abandoned their LWOP provisions for juveniles, and the Supreme Court struck down LWOP sentences for juveniles convicted of non-homicide offences. Nevertheless, the numbers currently in the system are striking. As of 2014, there were almost 50,000 LWOP prisoners in the United States, an astonishing number when compared with the figures in England, Australia, or the Netherlands, all of which had fewer than a hundred such prisoners at that time. Finally, as with the population on death row, LWOP prisoners are far more likely to be non-White. Across the US over two-thirds of the LWOP prisoners are non-White.

Courts around the world are coming to recognize that detention for the duration of a person's life may be inhumane. In 2013, the European Court of Human Rights ruled that European Union member states must allow some provision for natural life prisoners to be considered for release. The idea is that even the prisoners convicted of the worst murders should have the possibility of a review of their detention after having served, say, thirty years in prison. They would not necessarily be released, but some authority should at least take a look at their case, and hear any appeal they might have for release on parole. It seems likely that one day the US will go the same route. The US Supreme

Court has already ruled that LWOP for juveniles constitutes cruel and unusual punishment. My guess is that one day LWOP for adult offenders will be declared unconstitutional too.

The crimes that lead to imprisonment

Most countries try to reserve prison for offenders who represent a physical threat or who have committed a crime so serious that no lesser sentence—a fine, a period of unpaid work, a term of probation—is adequate. That makes sense in theory, but in practice it doesn't quite work out that way. Large numbers of prisoners are serving time for non-violent offences. Half the prisoners in the US were convicted of a non-violent crime and the percentage of non-violent prisoners is almost as high in other countries. Why were they sent to prison?

There are several explanations for the high percentage of non-violent prisoners in institutions designed primarily for offenders considered dangerous. First, someone with a long string of prior crimes will often be sent to prison not so much because the most recent theft is serious, but because he keeps committing crimes. Property crimes are more likely to be committed by repeat offenders, and so these individuals are more likely to be sent to prison. The second cause of non-violent admissions to prison is that many countries, especially the US, have mandatory sentencing laws—a court must impose prison if the offender has been convicted of a particular crime. Many drug offences in the US carry a mandatory sentence and approximately one prisoner in five is serving time for a drug offence. Finally, judges do not necessarily see prison as reserved for those who pose a serious threat to society or for those convicted of a crime of exceptional seriousness. Views will vary widely on the kinds of offences and offenders which merit imprisonment even if they don't pose a serious threat to society. A good example might be the protester who jumped into the Thames and disrupted the 2012 Oxford versus Cambridge boat race. The event was delayed and (even worse) Cambridge won the re-started race. He was sentenced to six months in prison. Even fans of this sporting event might struggle to see that young man as a threat to society. Clearly, prison is not just for the dangerous.

Repeat business: 'you again!'

The title of this chapter captures the paradox of contemporary prisons: we incarcerate people to stop them offending and yet back they come, having committed further crimes. Imprisonment punishes effectively, yet does little to change prisoners into law-abiding citizens. Most prisoners will re-offend at some point after they leave prison; as a result many will be re-admitted to custody. Young ex-prisoners are more likely to return than older prisoners; men more likely than female prisoners to be re-admitted; and offenders with drug and employment problems are the most likely to return of all the prisoners. The 'revolving door' of the prison is a universal feature of all CJSs. It has generated much speculation and research into the causes of re-offending—and how prison programmes can prevent this recidivism.

Populist politicians usually explain high recidivism rates by arguing that prison life is too easy. They claim that if the conditions of confinement were worse, ex-prisoners would work harder to avoid re-conviction and subsequent re-admission to prison. The media pick up on this theme and gleefully publish stories suggesting prisons are easy on prisoners. I once worked in a prison in a town called Milton. Because it had good sports facilities the papers dubbed it the 'Milton Hilton', and this led to calls for cutbacks to the facilities.

This view of prison life has led to calls for more austerity in prison, as though prisons were four star hotels and the management has decided they could function just as well if facilities were more modest. There is an attractive logic to the reasoning: we all avoid returning to a place where we were poorly treated—whether it's a harsh boarding school run by tyrannical teachers or a 'Fawlty Towers' style hotel. So the argument is: cut back on the prison food budget, cut out the recreational facilities, and restrict prisoners' visits—then fewer prisoners will return following re-conviction.

Regrettably for the theory, there is no evidence that nastier prisons reduce re-offending rates. One reason is that the causes of re-offending—like the causes of offending more generally—lie outside the CJS. Prison programmes may help prepare a prisoner for a law-abiding lifestyle but their impact will be modest. It will be far more important whether the ex-prisoner has a job to go to when he is released or a supportive family. The most common factors associated with re-offending are the absence of supportive social networks, weak or non-existent family relationships, unemployment, and unsuitable accommodation. Being homeless or in temporary accommodation before going to prison is a strong predictor of re-offending upon release. The CJS can do little to address these issues.

Politicians' calls for harsher prison conditions are also out of step with public opinion, even in the US, where the public tends to be more punitive towards offenders. When American politicians advocated a return to the use of prisoners to break rocks (as was the case in the old days) community opposition was apparent, and the proposals were abandoned. Making prison life harsher may also be counter-productive; it may breed resentment in prisoners, which leads to more crime after release. Harsh prisons are also more dangerous places for prisoners and their guards; a common cause of prison disturbances (including riots) is a sudden or unjustified change in conditions—such as a reduction in recreational facilities. Investing resources in prison conditions and rehabilitation programmes is not a case of making life easier for prisoners. It's an effective way of ensuring prisoners are less likely to offend when they leave the prison.

Why don't prisons rehabilitate?

Several factors limit the effectiveness of prison to change offenders. First, you can't change people overnight. The average sentence in the UK is around twelve months, of which the prisoner will serve six in prison and the remainder in the community. In other European countries the average prison sentence is even shorter. Most offenders admitted to prison have multiple problems associated with their offending. These usually include drug or alcohol addiction or abuse. In other Western countries such as Denmark, Sweden, and France the vast majority of prison sentences are six months or less. Six months is simply not enough time for the prison system to identify a prisoner's needs, and then devise and deliver remedial health, education, or employment-related programmes. If the prisoner has a mental health problem—and many do—the opportunities for therapy within even a well-resourced prison system are very limited. One prison I worked in had only one psychologist for hundreds of inmates; it was a question of 'take a number and wait'. Effective psychotherapy is out of the question with this kind of therapist to patient ratio.

The other barriers to rehabilitation are fiscal and scientific. We know a lot more about what works in terms of rehabilitating offenders now. Research by correctional psychologists and criminologists demonstrates that if prison programmes focus on addressing the specific *needs* and *risk* factors of individual prisoners, re-offending can be prevented. But rehabilitation is not an exact science and it is still hard to determine which interventions will be most effective.

Prison programmes—of an educational, vocational, or therapeutic nature—are seldom popular with politicians. The consequence is that when looking for ways to cut the costs of criminal justice, prison programmes and facilities top the list of targets. Remedial education programmes in prison are often the first casualty of correctional budget cuts. Libraries in prison are seldom that useful or well-provisioned. Another prison I worked in had a large and well-stocked library, yet it always seemed deserted. I finally asked the librarian why there were no prisoners reading or browsing, and she told me that they had no access to the library. If they knew the title of a specific book, they could request it be sent to their cells. Imagine running a public or university library that way.

Prison education is important; one of the best predictors of juvenile offending is poor academic performance. Delivering or pursuing education in prison is not easy, but it pays dividends. I once taught a university seminar in which one of the students was a prisoner. Rick attended class on a day pass from prison, accompanied by a prison officer. The guard would occasionally fall asleep during the lecture, but Rick never dozed. He successfully finished the course and ultimately completed two university degrees while serving time. After his release from prison he launched an exemplary career helping young offenders and former prisoners to re-adjust to life in open society. That's just one success story, but the statistics show clearly that gaining an education in prison will enhance a prisoner's chance of going straight after their release.

The bottom line on prisons

In modern society, prisons are as necessary as hospitals or schools; incarceration is a universal feature of criminal justice. Some offenders represent such a high risk to the safety of others that detention in a secure facility is necessary. Think of Timothy McVeigh and Terry Nichols, the offenders responsible for the Oklahoma bombing. Their crime cost 168 lives and caused almost half a billion dollars of damage to property. Or Ian Huntley, who killed two children in England.

There will also always be people who commit crimes of such seriousness that imprisonment is unavoidable, even if the offender no longer represents a danger to society. Think Myra Hindley in the UK or Karla Homolka in Canada—both women were complicit in the abduction and murder of children. With their murderous accomplices in prison for life, these women represented no further threat to other children; however, they were put in prison because of the harm they had already inflicted, not the harm they might inflict. Similarly, Bernard Madoff (who had perpetrated an investment fraud which defrauded thousands of their life savings) represented no physical threat to society. Neither, after exposure and conviction, was he any further threat to people's money. Yet the magnitude of his crimes, which had resulted in the financial ruin of many individuals, made long-term imprisonment inevitable. He was sentenced to serve 150 years.

One final statistic about prisons takes us back to the comparison with a four star hotel. Such hotels do share a feature with prison: cost. In England today, it costs approximately £38,000 ($60,000) to house one prisoner for a year. That sum would pay for a room in the Randolph, an elegant Oxford hotel, for the same period. For this reason alone, it is important to ensure that no-one is sent to prison unless it is absolutely necessary; it simply costs too much for what it offers as a response to crime. Contemporary prisons contain many people convicted of minor crimes, who do not represent a threat to the community. These people need to be punished *and* rehabilitated. Our prisons do a good job of punishing but fail to change prisoners for the better. The cost of this failure is more crime, more victims, more prisons, and bigger prison bills.

Release from prison

Almost all prisoners will be released from custody and most will finish their sentence in the community under some form of supervised release. If an offender is sentenced to three years' imprisonment, how long should he spend inside? Some people would say 'three years—what else?' Isn't it like asking how much money an offender ordered to pay a £500 fine should hand over to the State? The parallel is misplaced. The concept of allowing prisoners to spend the last part of their sentence in the community goes back a long way; it is one of the oldest features of criminal justice. This near universality shows that there is good reason to see merit in early release schemes. In practice, almost all prison regimes allow most prisoners to spend the last part of their prison sentence in the community—and this relates, as we will now see, to prisoners' rehabilitation.

Parole

Many countries operate a *discretionary parole* scheme—the prisoner has to apply to a parole board for permission to complete his sentence in the community. The inmate must make a case for release, documenting his progress in prison, his plans for living and employment upon release, and so forth. The parole board then considers two principal questions: is the inmate likely to commit further crimes if released on parole; and is his rehabilitation more likely if he is released on parole?

As with probation, there has been a shift in the orientation of parole. In the last century parole was seen as a right of prisoners, and the parole authorities were very much rehabilitation-oriented. More recently, both probation and parole have become more concerned about risk than rehabilitation. Release on parole is seen more as a privilege accorded to few prisoners, and only those for whom the risk of re-offending is demonstrably low. This more conservative approach to granting release on parole can be seen by examining the risk assessments conducted by parole board members. Prior to taking a decision on an application a parole board will classify the prisoner as low, medium, or high risk—a classification that will determine whether or not the prisoner is granted early release on parole. Parole authorities use interviews and risk prediction tools to classify prisoners. A review of such classifications in the UK found that over 90 per cent of prisoners who had been classified as being at high risk to re-offend did not in fact go on to commit another offence after their release. In other words, many of them could have been (and should have been) released early on parole.

The parole board has the discretion to decide whether the prisoner will be released before his sentence fully ends; if so, when and under what conditions of parole. For example, the board may authorize his release but order him to avoid visiting the neighbourhood in which the victim of his crime resides. Making release decisions is far from easy; how do you know whether the prisoner is a low or high risk to re-offend? The evidence put forward on his behalf may conflict with the position of the prison authorities.

In previous years parole board members tended to be political appointees who were susceptible to external pressure and bad publicity. If an offender serving his sentence on parole committed a serious crime, the media storm generated would make parole board members more conservative in future releasing decisions. Nowadays parole decisions are more professional and systematic; parole authorities consider risk factors and they benefit from the latest research in predicting who is likely to re-offend.

Against parole

A common parole eligibility point is when one-third of the sentence has been served. This means that an offender with a nine-year sentence may well be released shortly after serving just three years, if the board approves his parole application. Some people see this as undercutting the original sentence. In addition, critics argue that parole can be unfair—two inmates both sentenced to nine years may serve very different sentences if one receives the green light for release while the other is denied parole.

Parole decision-making can be unpredictable and dependent on the personalities of the board members. If one prisoner is released while another with a similar profile is denied parole, this will engender perceptions of unfairness. Indeed, surveys of prisoners often show that some prisoners regard the system as unfair, and consequently don't bother to apply for release—they just wait out their sentence and leave at the end of it. Many US states have abolished parole simply to ensure all detainees are treated equally in this regard. Perceptions of fairness are very important throughout the CJS. If defendants, offenders, or in this case prisoners believe that the system is unfair, it will also be seen to lack legitimacy. A CJS that lacks legitimacy—either from the perspective of the general public or from that of those most affected (the offenders)—will ultimately fail. For this reason, countries which retain discretionary release on parole have formalized parole hearings considerably. This means ensuring due process requirements are met. For example, a parole board must disclose to the prisoner any information it has about his case in order to permit him to respond. This is the equivalent of the requirement on the prosecutor to disclose the evidence against an accused prior to trial.

Some members of the public oppose parole or early release programmes on the grounds that they believe inmates who are still dangerous are being released into the community. This perception is largely created by rare tragedies in which a person recently released on parole commits a very serious crime of violence. Statistics contradict this public apprehension: almost all parolees complete their sentences in the community without committing additional crimes. When a parole officer revokes the parole of an offender and returns him to prison this is almost always for a breach of some technical condition.

The benefits of parole

Parole is not just 'time off' the sentence. Prisoners serving their sentences in the community must comply with requirements such as reporting to a parole officer and maintaining employment, and they can be recalled to prison if they violate their conditions. Herein lies the utility of parole: the supervision they receive on re-entering the community. A parolee who seems to be going off the rails—drinking heavily, failing to look for work, associating with known offenders—can be recalled to prison *before* this behaviour leads him to re-offend. Prison regimes which require prisoners to spend all of their time in prison are generally less effective at preventing re-offending—and they are more expensive than prisons which allow some kind of release before the sentence ends.

The incentive of early release encourages good behaviour in prison. Inmates who commit crimes or who violate prison rules can be denied parole or denied 'early release' credit. When early release is accompanied by supervision in the community by a parole officer—who performs the same function as a probation officer—it can assist in the prisoner's transition back to society. A CJS which requires an offender to serve every day of his nine-year sentence and then releases him 'cold turkey' onto the streets makes no sense. Prisoners would emerge unprepared for life on the outside.

There are other benefits associated with parole. Allowing prisoners to earn their release early also saves the CJS money: a six-year prison sentence served in full will cost society approximately £200,000 (US$300,000). On the other hand, if the offender spends the first half in prison and the second half living in the community under supervision, the cost will be closer to £120,000 (US$180,000), a considerable saving. The financial benefits of releasing prisoners early to be supervised in the community also include the income tax they will pay—most parolees are obliged to find work—whereas in prison they just cost the State money.

Another advantage of allowing a prisoner to serve part of his prison sentence in the community is that his dependants and partner are better off when they see him every day rather than just once a month on prison visits. When an offender is sent to prison, his family also suffer. This is one of the key weaknesses of imprisonment as a punishment. If the offender is ordered to pay a fine, or compensation to the victim, or made to work for free, his family is relatively unaffected. But when a court sends a mother to prison for eighteen months, her children are deprived of maternal care and become secondary victims. Without a mother, or with only one parent, family and school life become more challenging for the children; it increases their risk of truancy, academic failure, and, ultimately, juvenile delinquency. In this way the sins of the mother are visited on her children. This is another reason why the CJS strives to avoid imprisoning offenders unless it is absolutely necessary.

Early release schemes save a great deal of money, and this explains why, despite all the criticism, few jurisdictions have abandoned the practice. If a country which had been allowing prisoners to apply for parole at one-third of their sentence then abolished that parole, the costs of the prison estate would skyrocket. Abolishing early release would only be fiscally prudent if it was accompanied by a reduction in sentence lengths—avoiding an increase in the amount of time prisoners served inside. Reducing the length of prison sentences is unlikely to happen because it would be impossible to sell to the public—and politicians are generally only interested in criminal justice policies which are popular. Only the US has drastically curtailed early release from prison, by abolishing parole in many states or requiring prisoners to serve up to 85 per cent of their sentence before release.

Some form of early release scheme makes sense. The prospect of getting out of jail before the sentence ends incentivizes the inmate to take courses or employment training programmes. It would be a very strange prison which conveyed to inmates the message that whatever they do in prison, they all get out when the sentence of the court expires, and never before. If we want offenders to change then we need to provide them with opportunities and incentives. Employment training, remedial education, and other prison programmes constitute the opportunities; parole, the incentive.

Where do the public stand on the controversial practice of parole? Most people support the *principle* of early release from prison but appear to condemn the *practice* in their particular jurisdiction. But much of the negative public reaction to parole can be explained by adverse media coverage and misinformation. People assume that every prisoner gets parole, and at the first application. In reality only a minority are granted parole and often only after several applications. More anxiety-provoking is the belief of many in society that prisoners released on parole are dangerous and represent a threat to the community. In reality, as noted, only a small percentage of offenders on parole are returned to prison, and then usually for violation of a technical condition rather than for committing a new crime. Providing people with information changes their attitudes.

The effect of information on public attitudes

In one study we gave members of the public a parole application to consider and asked them to decide whether the prisoner should be granted release or denied parole. One-half of the sample was given factual information about parole (the 'informed' group). For example, they were informed about the kinds of conditions imposed on paroled prisoners and the consequences for the prisoner of breaking these rules. The other half were simply asked to make a decision to grant or deny release based on their own existing views (the 'uninformed' group of subjects). The results of this experiment were clear. Reactions to the parole application were very different in the two groups. Three-quarters of the 'informed' group favoured releasing the prisoner on parole, compared to less than half of the other group. The study suggested that, when properly informed about the conditions and effects of parole on prisoners, members of the public are significantly more likely to be in favour of supervised, early release from prison on parole.

There is a more general lesson here: since the public gets almost all its information about criminal justice from the news media, most people are misinformed about many aspects of justice. So when an opinion poll suggests that most people are in favour of capital punishment or opposed to parole, we need to bear in mind that this opinion may not be based on facts and that it might change if efforts were made to give the general public accurate information. The best research into public opinion will give people sufficient information about an area of criminal justice, and then it will explore their views. When this happens, the public are far more thoughtful and sophisticated in their reasoning.

Home confinement: the virtual prison

The growing interest in risk management throughout the CJS has also played a role in managing offenders at home through more intensive forms of electronic monitoring. New surveillance technologies have opened the door to managing risk in the community. House arrest accompanied by electronic monitoring has emerged as a highly visible feature of what has been termed the 'new age of surveillance'. Home incarceration would have been inconceivable without the means of ensuring offender compliance. The most recent developments include global positioning systems (GPS) which permit the State to monitor the movements of offenders beyond the confines of their residences. These technologies have increased the appeal of community sanctions by addressing public concerns about the risk posed by offenders to the community.

This sentence exists in many nations although it goes under different names such as community custody and home detention. The common element is that these offenders serve a sentence of custody at home, with the threat of institutional confinement hanging over their heads should they fail to comply with their conditions. The presence of the threat explains the many references to the legend of the 'Sword of Damocles'. Damocles was a courtier forced by a tyrant to remain motionless while sitting under a sharp sword that was hanging by a thread. One careless movement would result in rather unpleasant consequences for the man. The tyrant was singularly unpopular and wanted to show what it was like to live under constant threat of death (he had been the object of numerous assassination attempts).

Whether home confinement is appropriate for offenders convicted of the most serious crimes is very contentious; in most Western jurisdictions the use of this sentence in such cases is likely to provoke widespread public opposition and negative media coverage. This explains in part why some CJSs exclude certain offences from consideration for this kind of sanction.

Victims often approach community custody with considerable scepticism. Many victims come to court with little knowledge of sentencing trends, and expectations that most offenders convicted of a crime of violence spend significant periods in custody. It may come as an unpleasant surprise to the victim when the court rejects the victim's (or prosecutor's) plea to impose a lengthy prison term and instead imposes a term of community custody, permitting the offender to resume living at home. Home confinement sanctions represent a useful additional option in the sentencer's toolbox. They cost much less than custody and offenders are spared many of the destructive effects of imprisonment. Home confinement sanctions remain a sideshow however; some countries do not have a form of this sentence. Those CJSs that do have one typically use it for only a small percentage of offenders who would otherwise be sent to a prison.

Life in the virtual prison

What is it like to live under a tight set of court-ordered conditions, including house arrest or a strict curfew? Much will depend upon the nature of those restrictions as well as the length of time that they have to be observed. Many offenders claim that living under home confinement conditions was harder and the conditions more intrusive than they had anticipated. The most difficult part of serving a community custody sentence is complying with house arrest or a very restrictive curfew. Many of the home confinement offenders I interviewed had been sentenced to twenty-four-hour house arrest. The consequences of this condition included: no participation in social activities; family outings and special occasions were affected; the embarrassment when other people realized that the individual was serving a sentence. The most punitive element of home confinement for these offenders was the impact that the sentence had upon their children, whose interactions with their parents and daily lives were affected for the duration of the sentence. One female offender discussed the house arrest condition in the context of other conditions imposed: 'the absolute curfew is the hardest thing. I can't go anywhere without telling my PO [probation officer]. Absolute curfew is like house arrest. My daughter wants to go the park, but I can't take her.' However, she added that she would rather stay at home and be with her kids, and she believed that if she had not had kids she would have been sent to jail. Home confinement is supposed to be an alternative to prison, so it cannot be experienced as being much easier than prison. Furthermore, if home confinement could be used more often, it would save the CJS a lot of money—but it must still impose a sufficient punishment on offenders.

Life after release

Except for the offenders serving life sentences, all sentences end with the expiry of the court order. Once the offender has complied with the conditions of a community order, paid the fine, or completed the sentence of imprisonment (including any time on parole), the sentence will end. However, the shadow of the CJS will remain upon the offender's life.

Ex-offenders do not easily or expeditiously regain their status as full members of society. All jurisdictions impose restrictions on their employment, residential, or mobility rights. For example, sex offenders may be placed on a sex offender registry. Offenders convicted of a criminal offence will be obliged in many employment contexts to declare that they have a criminal record. These restrictions, some of which may be reasonable, others less so, have important impacts on offenders' life prospects. Voluntary agencies routinely vet applications for criminal convictions. Anything which undermines an ex-offender's ability to find employment is particularly damaging, since stable employment is one of the best predictors of desistance.

Societies vary greatly in the range of restrictions they place on ex-offenders. The US is particularly unforgiving. For example, offenders convicted of a felony are denied the vote as a result of felony disenfranchisement laws, which lead to the exclusion of hundreds of thousands of citizens. All US states permit ex-offenders to regain their voting rights, but the procedures are so time-consuming and cumbersome that few people benefit from having their right to vote restored. The numbers are staggering and have important consequences for a democratic society. Approximately six million Americans have temporarily or permanently lost their right to vote as a result of a criminal conviction. And, as with so many other elements of criminal justice in the US, this post-sentence punishment falls most heavily on Black Americans, who have been disenfranchised at a much higher rate than White Americans. Well over two million Black Americans were unable to vote in the 2010 US presidential election. As with some other punitive features of criminal justice in the US, this is slowly changing. A number of states have softened their felony disenfranchisement laws. In Nebraska, for example, felons are now denied the right to vote for only two years after the sentence ends, rather than for life.

Escaping a criminal past

Most CJSs have created schemes which permit ex-offenders to apply for a pardon for their convictions. After a number of years have passed, the individual applies to have his record cleared: if he is found to have led a law-abiding life since his sentence ended the conviction is removed from the criminal record database. Laws which permit offenders to shake off their past are very important; without them the consequences of a criminal conviction would never end. Rehabilitation is much harder when you still carry the burden of a conviction. The ability to erase a conviction and start again is particularly relevant for young adults. Many people in their late teens or early adulthood make mistakes, make criminal decisions. Having paid the price for their offending they should be encouraged to regain the full rights and responsibilities of citizenship.

Criminal records should be kept only for as long as is absolutely necessary. Some people subscribe to the view 'once an offender, always an offender'. Yet the statistics show that the vast majority of offenders either 'age out' of a period of criminality, usually in their twenties, or take steps towards rehabilitation which prevent a return to crime. Criminal justice resembles marriage as it used to be: it was relatively easy to get married, but very hard to get divorced. A criminal conviction is the same today: many people can acquire one relatively easily. It has been estimated that approximately one adult male in four acquires a criminal conviction by the time he is 40 years old—and once acquired, a criminal record is hard to shake off, sometimes re-emerging years later. It should be the other way round. We should make it hard to acquire a criminal conviction—many incidents of antisocial behaviour which are now prosecuted as crimes could be dealt with without recourse to the CJS. Once an offender has served his sentence we should encourage him to take the necessary steps towards desistance, and when this is achieved he should be regarded as a citizen with full civic rights.

Chapter 6
Hearing the crime victim?

Thirty years ago someone broke into my home late at night, stealing and damaging some property. Months passed after I had reported the crime to the police, I eventually went to give evidence at the trial of the man accused of the burglary. In fact, I went to court twice, only to be sent home on both occasions, having been told that the matter had been 'put over'—delayed for some reason that was never explained to me. On the third visit, after passing hours in the waiting area, a prosecutor came over, said, 'You can go, the case has been resolved', and disappeared before I could ask any questions. I never knew what had happened to the person charged, nor did I have the opportunity to describe the effect of the crime to the prosecutor or the judge. It didn't seem right that the person most affected by the crime had so little information about—or input into—the criminal justice response.

Why were victims treated in this way? One explanation takes us back to the models of justice.

Finding a role for the victim

The adversarial model has historically paid little attention to the crime victim, who plays a greater role in inquisitorial systems of justice. For example, in Germany the crime victim benefits from a legal right to be represented at the trial—the victim becomes an official 'party' to the proceeding. In contrast, crime victims pose a problem for the two-party system of adversarial justice. Within the adversarial model of justice, a criminal trial is construed as a conflict between two equal adversaries—the State and the defendant—played out before an impartial adjudicator—the judge.

The victim often serves as the principal witness for the prosecution, and having served this function has no further role to play in criminal proceedings. The victim is not 'represented' by the prosecutor the way that the accused is represented by his lawyer. On this traditional model, the victim remains out in the cold. This side-lining of the victim led to widespread criticism of the criminal justice system (CJS), and much dissatisfaction on the part of crime victims. It was from this dissatisfaction with the CJS response that the victims' movement emerged.

My experience at court was typical of the way that criminal justice responded to victims in the 1980s. Surveys of crime victims demonstrated that many crimes were never reported to the police, often because victims were apprehensive about how they would be treated. Studies also showed that victims and witnesses were 'uncooperative' with respect to prosecutorial efforts to bring offenders to justice because they were intimidated by the CJS or were uninformed as to what was expected of them.

Contact with criminal justice professionals made victims more, not less, critical of the CJS. The experience of being called to testify as a witness, cross-examination by lawyers, and the lack of contact with the prosecutor led to many victims becoming disillusioned. Part of the problem was the attitudes of police and prosecutors. These professionals were seldom positive or respectful. Families of homicide victims told me that they had received notification of the death of their loved one over the telephone—the police didn't even send an officer to the family residence with the tragic news. If relatives of a murder victim have experienced such cavalier treatment, imagine how victims of less serious crimes were treated.

Contrast this with the experiences of another kind of victim: people injured in a road accident and subsequently admitted to hospital for treatment. Surveys of patients generally reveal dissatisfaction with delays in receiving treatment, but high levels of satisfaction with their care and the medical professionals once treatment began. For victims of criminal justice the opposite was the case: increased contact with criminal justice *lowered* ratings of satisfaction with the system and the people who operate it.

Today, much has changed. The additional attention paid and services offered to crime victims represent the most striking change in justice over this period. Most of today's victim-related reforms began in the US and then spread to other common law countries. Crime victims now enjoy a range of services and rights. Victim–witness units exist in all Western CJSs and provide a range of services to crime victims—from first contact with the police through to the sentencing of the offender. Victims are notified when hearings are scheduled so that they do not have to wait in court unnecessarily. CJSs consider the welfare of the victim to a much greater extent, including adopting changes to the physical environment. In many courthouses, separate waiting rooms are provided for defence and State witnesses, unlike in the past, when victims and accused persons often came into close contact at the courthouse.

The role of the victim has been transformed from passive witness to active participant, with rights for input into proceedings. While still lacking full 'standing' as a party to the proceedings, victims in the US, Canada, England, or Australia, are consulted, informed, and allowed to provide input into criminal justice. To some, this evolution represents a threat to core values central to the adversarial model. Victims' rights advocates, on the other hand, view the new privileges (and powers) of the victim as evidence of progress.

Most countries provide victims with the right to receive information about the status of the case in which they are involved (in the US, referred to as *victim notification* laws), the right to apply for and receive financial and psychological assistance, and input rights throughout the criminal process (such as in bail, sentencing, and parole hearings). Although most of these rights and benefits have been generally accepted, the right to provide input into sentencing decisions has proved controversial. Controversies revolve around the extent and forms of victim input, and its impact on the principles and outcomes of criminal justice proceedings.

In the US, victims' input rights have also assumed a constitutional dimension. The Victims' Rights Amendment is a proposed amendment to the US Constitution that would establish various rights for crime victims nationwide with remedies in cases of non-compliance by legal professionals. These rights include the right to speak during the course of legal proceedings, including bail, plea bargains, sentencing, and parole. As yet, the proposed Victims' Rights Amendment has failed to gain the necessary number of states in support, but the public are clearly onside: 90 per cent of the public indicated they would support such an amendment. The principal argument against its passage has been that victim participation and input can be accomplished by enforcing existing laws.

Elsewhere, many countries have adopted 'Victims' Charters', which attempt to ensure that victims receive assistance and are informed of their rights. For example, in England and Wales there is a Code of Practice for Crime Victims. This regulates the kinds of services that should be offered victims and ensures that their *service rights* are respected. A range of victim-oriented organizations such as Victim Support deliver services to crime victims and actively lobby the government on behalf of crime victims. Victim Support assists approximately two million crime victims every year. Finally, the importance of victim participatory rights is apparent from Article 68 of the Rome Statute of the International Criminal Court (ICC), which recognizes the security interests and participatory rights of victims and witnesses, and allows victims to provide input into sentencing decisions at the international level.

Categories of crime victim

What do crime victims want from the CJS? Let's consider three general categories of victims. One group wants nothing to do with the CJS because the crime was a personal matter; or they have resolved it themselves; or they have been reimbursed for loss by their insurance company. These are the *silent victims* for whom the CJS is required to do little.

A second group seek information, compensation, and services, but not to participate: *passive victims*, whose needs the CJS is required to address. They want to be told about developments (such as when the case is coming to trial), when the offender is being sentenced, and when he is coming up for release from prison. The CJS responds to this group through victim services agencies. Victims are also provided with services—counselling for trauma perhaps, or compensation and assistance in making applications.

Receiving compensation may well be more important to the victim than ensuring the offender is punished. It may be reassuring, possibly even *satisfying*, to see the offender punished, but most of us placed in a similar position would rather receive adequate compensation for our losses. A key objective of criminal justice is therefore obtaining compensation for the crime victim. One way of achieving this is through the courts at sentencing. Compensation through criminal justice is controversial to some people who believe that the sentence should focus on imposing punishment, and not on compensating the victim.

When an offender is sentenced for a crime, the court may order him to compensate the victim for: personal injury; financial losses as a result of theft or criminal damage; loss of income (if the victim had to stop working as a result of the crime); and other expenses related to the crime. The offender is ordered to take steps to rectify some of the harm caused. Most countries operate criminal injury compensation schemes. In England and Wales, victims may apply for compensation under the Criminal Injuries Compensation Scheme. These schemes permit crime victims to receive financial compensation without waiting for the court to order the offender to provide it. All this makes a lot of sense to crime victims as well as to members of the public. Studies have shown that given a choice between achieving compensation for the victim and punishing the offender, the public and crime victims see compensation as being more important.

Simply providing information about case developments is not enough for some of these victims; they want to understand *why* decisions are taken by the legal professionals. Prosecutors make many of the decisions of greatest concern to victims. For example, the prosecution may have decided that it was not in the public interest to prosecute the suspect. This failure to prosecute may trouble the crime victim. Or the prosecutor may charge the accused with a less serious crime than the one the victim believes was actually committed. Or the prosecution may decide not to appeal a sentence which to the victim seems too lenient.

I recall a case of homicide in which the killing had taken place on an escalator in a busy shopping centre. CCTV footage in the news media of a knife-wielding assailant, along with witnesses' statements to the press, gave everyone the impression that the accused had clearly intended to kill the victim—it seemed an open and shut case of murder. Imagine then the reaction of the victim's family when the prosecutor agreed to a plea bargain: the accused pleaded guilty to a less serious crime—manslaughter—rather than murder. This meant the offender would serve two to three years in prison, not imprisonment for life. No explanation was offered, so the victim's parents were left scratching their heads, convinced that justice had been denied their son. This case underlined the importance of giving reasons for decisions to victims and their families, particularly in serious cases such as this one. Traditionally, legal professionals have been reluctant to explain their decisions: judges point to their published judgments, and prosecutors usually offer no comment. That is now changing; CJSs are being required to become more accountable and part of this accountability means offering explanations.

Many CJSs now require their prosecutors to explain their decisions to the victim—such as whether the sentence imposed should be appealed. Some systems go even further and insist that prosecutors consult the victim before taking decisions. This requirement is seldom popular with prosecutors and you can see why. They are trying to discharge their duties and don't want to be blown off course by a victim who may, if consulted, insist on a different course of action. There is also the danger of raising false expectations; the victim may feel that having been consulted, his opinion should decide the matter. When this turns out not to be the case, the victim may feel worse than if he had not been consulted in the first place.

The participatory victim

The third category of victim—the *active victims*—represents a greater challenge for the adversarial CJS. Active victims want to participate in CJS decision-making. They seek to express their views when the accused applies for bail, and want to offer an opinion when sentencing takes place, or when he applies for release from prison on parole. Victims' advocates argue that the victim has a right to make representations at key stages of the criminal process. These are usually referred to as *procedural* rights—as distinguished from the *service* rights described earlier.

The problematic nature of allowing victims to provide input is obvious. If, at the request of the victim, the court denies bail to

113

the accused, the prosecution has become a private rather than public matter—a case of one individual (the victim) against another (the alleged perpetrator). There are also problems in terms of expertise and fairness. Crime victims are unfamiliar with the criteria and grounds for granting bail or for releasing the prisoner on parole. Nor are they well informed about things like the appropriate sentence lengths for different crimes. If victims decide or even influence the decision at bail, sentencing, or parole, then fairness may fly out of the window. It would be unfair, within a system of State justice, to punish an offender according to the extent their victim wishes. This would mean some offenders might be treated lightly, having been lucky enough to rob a forgiving victim, while robbers who had been less lucky and robbed a more vindictive person might find themselves paying a disproportionate price for their crimes, simply because punishment was based on their victim's reactions.

So what's the answer? Should we keep the active victim firmly in the background, standing by to testify at trial and then to be dismissed? Adversarial criminal justice has evolved a compromise position. The principal vehicle to accommodate their desire for input is known as the *victim impact statement* (VIS). These statements originated in the US in the 1980s, and then proliferated around the Western world.

Victim impact statements

Victims are allowed to submit a statement which is then used to guide or inform decision-making throughout the CJS. The statement is supposed to contain legally relevant information about the case. It is usually a form which contains questions about the impact of the crime on the victim. The victim can also provide a description of the impact of the crime using their own words. Victims use the statement to provide details on the physical, psychological, social, and economic harm they have suffered as a result of the crime. This information will be used by the court at sentencing to help determine the seriousness of the offence.

For example, before the trial the victim might have information on the accused which is relevant to the bail decision. Did he threaten the victim with reprisals if the latter reported him to the police? Has he made threats in the past? A court contemplating release on bail will read the victim's words, and consider the matter—along with submissions from the accused applying for bail. Similarly for sentencing: there the task of a sentencing court is to impose a sentence which reflects the seriousness of the crime, and for this purpose these statements provide unique insight into the crime. For example, prosecutors or judges may not fully understand the effects of various crimes until the victims describe their experiences in detail.

Critics of victim impact statements argue that similar cases end up being disposed of differently, depending on the persuasiveness of the victim. Some legal scholars argue that victim input violates the fundamental principles of the adversarial legal system, which do not recognize the victim as a party to the proceedings. Including victims would transform the trial between the State and the defendant into a three-way proceeding (State–victim–offender). Such practices, it was argued, belong only in civil law systems, not in adversarial legal systems. Some people contend that victims may exaggerate the harm they sustained—to get more compensation or to ensure the judge imposes a harsher sentence. Victims may take advantage of the opportunity to criticize the offender or make allegations of other crimes that have not been charged. In responding to these critiques the CJS has introduced some checks and balances: quality control on victim input.

First, there are limits on the kind of material which should go into the statement; this should prevent victims from including prejudicial or irrelevant material. Second, the prosecutor may review the victim impact statement to make sure the victim has not written something improper—for example, making unfounded allegations about the offender in the case. Third, the offender's lawyer may decide to cross-examine the victim on the statement submitted to verify it is accurate: was the victim really off work for three months? Was the stolen watch really worth £500? In this way the CJS ensures that the victim impact statement contains useful information rather than just the victim's opinion.

Are victim impact statements beneficial?

Since victim impact statements are part of the CJS in almost all countries and much research has accumulated, we can draw some evidence-based conclusions about their usefulness. Although only a minority of victims choose to submit a statement, those that do tend to find the experience beneficial. Victims who depose statements are less likely to feel excluded from the criminal process, and more likely to leave court with a sense of closure. The most compelling evidence comes from responses to the question, '*Would you submit a statement again if you were victimized?*' This question has been posed to victims in several countries including the US, Canada, Australia, and the United Kingdom, and the result is consistent: most victims state that they would submit a statement in the event of future victimization. In some cases these statements also benefit the offender, who may not fully appreciate the harm he has caused until he hears directly from the victim. Research has shown that learning about the impact of crime on victims reduces the likelihood that the offender will re-offend.

Legal professionals are generally favourable to this limited form of input from the crime victim. Judges find the statements useful in terms of helping them understand the full impact—and hence seriousness—of the crime. The statement is particularly useful for crimes in which the impact on the victim was disproportionate or unusual, or involved a crime of violence, sex offences, or crimes in which property was stolen or damaged.

Defence lawyers are less positive about victim impact statements, perhaps because they are concerned that when the victim deposes a statement, their clients get treated more harshly. The statements can be quite emotional at times, and some have suggested that they may be overly influential as a result. The concern is probably misplaced; research shows that sentencing does not get tougher when the victim provides an impact statement. Judges are able to use the information contained in the victim impact statement without being influenced by its emotional tone.

If this all sounds very positive, it must be recalled that any criminal justice initiative, including victim impact schemes, can only benefit the CJS if criminal justice professionals deliver them effectively. In reality, police and other professionals charged with providing information about these schemes often fail to do so. In our research involving victims across England we found that less than one-third of crime victims recalled being offered the opportunity to complete a victim statement. So although a victim impact statement programme has been operating for over a decade in this country, only a minority of victims were informed of its existence and allowed to submit a statement. I doubt victims are treated much better in other countries with impact statement schemes operating. As with so many reforms, it is reliant on effective implementation.

Victim recommendations at sentencing and parole

Many US states permit (and some actually encourage) victims to recommend a specific sentence to the court. This is prohibited in all other jurisdictions on the grounds that victims are unlikely to have an accurate idea of the sentences imposed for different crimes. Practitioners and scholars generally oppose this practice on the grounds that it will lead to inconsistent and unfair sentencing.

Victims also are allowed to participate in parole hearings. Again, there is a gap between the US and other countries. Across the US, crime victims are often allowed to attend parole hearings, and to offer their opinion on whether the prisoner should be released. In all other countries victims are allowed only to submit an impact statement for the parole board to consider. They may attend the parole hearing, but not necessarily to speak to the board.

As with sentencing, if victims are allowed to influence the outcome (whether the prisoner is granted parole), this would be unfair. The general position that has been reached with respect to victims is that they should not be asked their opinion on what should happen to the offender. Victim input should be legally relevant to the decision being taken. Thus if the victim has been threatened by the accused currently being held in pre-trial detention, the authority deciding whether to release him should be aware of that threat—and the accused should have an opportunity to respond to the victim's allegation.

On the other hand, it is unlikely that the victim has relevant information for a parole board trying to decide whether to release the prisoner after he has served, say, eight years in prison. Normally, the victim has had no contact with the offender for years, and is not in a position to shed light on whether he represents a risk to the community. In terms of victim input then, the critical distinction here is between *information* and *opinion*. If the victim has *information* relevant to the decision, the parole board should listen to his submission. For example, the prisoner may have written threatening letters or in some other way contacted the victim. If the victim just wants to express an *opinion* ('the offender should be sent to prison for years after what he did to me') then this is not relevant to a State prosecution, and the victim's view should not be expressed to the judge.

Much progress has been made in improving the criminal justice response to victims. The latest victim surveys show higher rates of satisfaction with criminal justice than ever before. Victims are significantly more likely to report having been kept informed about case developments and are more likely to obtain compensation than in the past. In addition, a number of opportunities for providing input have arisen. Has criminal justice introduced sufficient reforms to adequately meet the needs of crime victims? The answer depends upon your perspective. Some argue that criminal justice in the adversarial CJS has still not gone far enough. They argue that the system found in English speaking countries should be replaced by the European system noted earlier, in which victims are full participants in the criminal justice process. Other victims' advocates claim that victims need more participatory rights throughout the CJS and that these rights need to be better enforced. Legal professionals counter that increasing the involvement and influence of the crime victim still further will distort the adversarial system beyond all recognition.

These changes to the status of the victim in the CJS are likely to stay; public support is stronger for victim-friendly reforms than for any other kind of innovation.

Another way that the victim has changed the face of criminal justice is through the growth of *restorative justice* (see Box 2). This is an alternative to criminal justice in which the emphasis is less on punishing the offender and more on restoring the social harmony which existed before the crime occurred. Victims are central to the many restorative justice programmes and initiatives that have sprung up around the world, particularly in Australia and New Zealand. These programmes are supported by the public, who see much merit in a scheme in which the offender makes amends rather than simply receiving a punishment.

In one test of the degree of public support for restorative justice, we gave a representative sample of the public two cases to consider involving young offenders who had broken into someone's home and taken property worth £500 (US$800). We asked them whether the offenders should be sent to prison or given a community order as part of a restorative justice solution. One offender had expressed remorse for the crime and promised to pay the homeowners back for their losses. Support for incarcerating the offender was much lower for this case than for the same crime but without any offer of compensation for the victim.

> ### Box 2 Alternative responses to crime: restorative justice and the fraudulent handyman
>
> Criminal justice represents only one possible response to crime. Imagine a handyman who defrauds several elderly clients. Tom charges them for repairs which are unnecessary or work that has not been performed. The total amount defrauded is £20,000. One response would involve a criminal prosecution. If convicted, Tom will probably be imprisoned for three to six months. A short prison sentence will do little to reform him. It may even make him more likely to re-offend. The criminal conviction will follow him for years and may restrict his employment opportunities, or travel or emigration plans (some employers will refuse to hire ex-offenders; some countries will not allow ex-offenders to visit or immigrate). The court could order the handyman to compensate his victims but this is unlikely to work out—most offenders spend their ill-gotten gains very quickly. The victims will probably never get their money back. An alternative approach involves restorative justice. The police convene a meeting between the victims and the handyman. At this meeting, Tom apologizes to the victims and explains why he stole their money. He might pay back some of the funds and offer some additional compensation. Both sides will profit from this arrangement: the victims get their money back (or some of it at least), an apology, and an explanation from the offender; and victims are often keen to get all three. Tom will not acquire a criminal record or go to prison. Society will benefit too. It will have saved the expense of prosecuting and punishing the offender. The costs in police time

to investigate, the prosecution of the case, a trial, followed by six months custody might cost the taxpayer £30,000 (US$50,000). Restorative justice programmes have emerged in all Western nations. And they have been found to work. Research in England, Australia, and Canada has demonstrated that restorative justice initiatives and programmes are often more beneficial to victims than criminal justice responses—particularly in cases involving juvenile offenders.

Chapter 7
The future of criminal justice

Predicting the direction of criminal justice is a perilous undertaking, although the evolution of criminal justice to date offers some clues to the future. A number of trends will continue. Western criminal justice is undergoing great transformation, in part because of the worldwide conditions of austerity created by the global economic recession of 2008–10. Western societies are committed to reducing the costs of public services, including criminal justice. Most likely this means more budget cuts, and more privatization.

There will be much greater public awareness and official scrutiny of police. Until the advent of mobile phones or CCTV, the work of the police was invisible. Now that almost everyone carries a phone with a camera, and with the prevalence of CCTV, police misconduct is far more likely to result in official action. Many police services are also equipping their officers with helmet cameras—to deter false allegations of abuse. These developments are also likely to deter officers from abusing their powers in the same way that electronic monitoring can deter offenders from re-offending.

The current level of imprisonment in countries such as the US and the UK is unsustainable in the long-term, and it is likely that many countries will seek to reduce the use of imprisonment as a sanction. Several US states are beginning to re-think their mandatory sentencing laws, having seen the prison costs that these trigger. Nothing focuses the mind of a legislature on reform quite so much as a huge budget deficit. Prison will become what we have always intended it to be, but which to date we have failed to achieve: a sanction of last resort for offenders whose liberty constitutes an unacceptable risk to the community (see Box 3). At present, only a minority of prisoners fit this description.

Box 3 The risk of risk

Perhaps the most significant development in criminal justice—and one which is likely to continue—concerns the management of risk. Whether in terms of deciding who to release on bail, sentence to custody, or release on parole, CJSs are becoming increasingly obsessed with trying to predict the individual's level of risk. Once this is determined, the decision then shapes the nature of the CJS response. Of course, all stages of criminal justice have long tried to reduce risk; more recently this has been accomplished through the use of predictive devices—scales which measure the offender's likelihood of re-offending. At sentencing, offenders are assigned a score based upon a number of variables such as their prior convictions, any substance abuse problems, and other factors associated with re-offending. This score is then used to help decide whether to commit them to prison, or order them to serve a sentence in the community. While it may sound reasonable to systematically identify an offender's risk level and then match this to appropriate interventions or treatments in prison, there are, nonetheless, worrying elements to the system. For example, these scales often 'over-predict', and low- to medium-risk offenders can end up receiving sentences that would be more appropriate for higher-risk individuals. In addition, some US states use demographic variables—over which the offender has

Box 3 Continued

no control—to help determine, for example, whether a prison sentence will be imposed. In one state, if an offender has a high enough score on the risk of re-offending scale, he is not entitled to receive a community penalty. The scale assigns points if the individual is male, and also if he is under 25. As a group, younger males carry a higher risk of re-offending than women or older male offenders. So if you are a young male, you are more likely to go to prison rather than receive a community penalty. The scales work like those of car insurance premiums, where fees are significantly higher for young male drivers because as a group they cause more accidents. Call me old fashioned, but that seems unfair—both for young male drivers and for male offenders. What's your view?

Electronic monitoring is the most likely candidate to replace custody as a sentence. A significant number of people are subject to electronic monitoring at present. The profile varies but includes high-risk accused released on bail; convicted offenders ordered to serve a term of home confinement; and prisoners released to serve the last part of their prison sentence in the community. More and more offenders will be ordered to serve a sentence of electronically monitored home confinement, and the CJS will impose a charge to cover the costs of the monitoring device. Other electronic forms of surveillance are likely to be developed which will permit the CJS to prevent crime without detention—knowing he is being constantly watched will be sufficient to deter many offenders before they are sent to prison. Databases will monitor an offender's whereabouts on a twenty-four-hour basis—this will have a greater deterrent effect than the prospect of possible imprisonment. An offender is unlikely to commit an offence if he knows the State is aware of his locations at all times. My guess is that the current high rates of re-offending will decline significantly, simply because we will have much greater control over offenders.

European states will make a much greater effort to punish offenders through financial penalties and asset seizure. At present, courts can confiscate property and seize assets, but usually only when the offender has been convicted of an offence involving organized crime, and the appropriated property is seized because it was purchased in whole or part by illegal funds arising from the proceeds of crime. In the future we shall see the CJS seizing property such as cars and high value goods more frequently—both as a punishment and also to generate income for the State. However, courts will have to regulate this policy, which could be subject to abuse. Asset or property forfeiture has long existed in the US, and has been problematic in some respects—for example, when the assets are forfeited to the local police, they can create an incentive to prosecute.

There is likely to be greater harmonization of criminal justice practices, as countries learn from experiences around the world regarding the most effective ways of achieving the goals of criminal justice, whether these involve policing or correctional treatment programmes. The increased political integration in Europe will lead to more uniform responses to offending. In the US the Model Penal Code project represents an important 'best practice' for the individual states. As a result of this project, legal academics and practitioners have developed a set of provisions to regulate sentencing and release. This package of provisions can then be applied across the country generating more principled and more uniform criminal justice. Europe may one day launch a similar initiative. As more nations join the EU, more will become subject to EU restrictions on penal practices such as the abolition of capital punishment.

Capital punishment remains a legal penalty in many nations but its days seem numbered. In fact, the use of capital punishment in Western criminal justice has been declining for centuries. First, the number of crimes for which an offender could be executed has been progressively restricted. Today, it is largely restricted to murder or treason in a time of war. Second, it was eliminated in cases involving a juvenile offender. Third, more and more countries have abolished capital punishment. As of 2014, only a small minority of countries retain the death penalty as a legal punishment. The list includes the US, Cuba, Iran, Saudi Arabia, Japan, India, China, and several Caribbean states.

This incongruous list suggests that different reasons exist for retention. In the US, capital punishment has survived due to a strong conservative streak in society resulting in punitive attitudes to offenders. In Iran, the Islamist government has protected the death penalty. Retention of the death penalty in the Caribbean states and Japan is harder to explain. One explanation for the progressive abolition of the death penalty around the world is political harmonization. When the EU voted to abolish the death penalty this applied to all member states. In addition, countries seeking EU membership must agree to abolish capital punishment as a condition of admission. Another pressure to replace death with life imprisonment has been studies showing racial bias in execution rates. These developments have had an impact on public opinion. Even in the US, where public support has traditionally been high, opposition to the death penalty has been growing. In 1994, approximately 80 per cent of the public supported capital punishment; twenty years later this had fallen to 60 per cent. It is likely to fall still further in the next few decades. As the number of botched executions, wrongful convictions, and international condemnation rises, the US may well re-think its capital punishment policies.

The victims' rights movement has not yet reached its peak. In all likelihood we shall see victims being given even more rights throughout the criminal process. This will call for some careful balancing of competing interests. Simply allowing victims more input and more control without careful consideration of the impact on fairness and the interests of defendants is a recipe for disaster. As with so many issues in the controversial field of criminal justice, it is a question of balance.

Appendix

Extract from the Court of Appeal judgment

'There are a number of features which obviously mitigate the offence...and we have largely set them out in our narrative account of the facts. We have recorded that the appellant has no sense of remorse for what she has done. In this particular case the absence of remorse does not extinguish the mitigation that she has already suffered and will continue hereafter to suffer the terrible grief of the loss of Thomas, as she would put it, as a result of the accident in July 2007. The mitigation consequent on her grief should not be reduced by the absence of remorse for the killing. She was ill equipped psychologically to cope with the disaster which befell Thomas, and for that reason, the consequent stresses and strains on an already fragile personality were disproportionately grave. In our view her mental responsibility for her actions, driven as she was by a compulsive obsession, was diminished if not sufficiently for the purposes of the defence of diminished responsibility, certainly to an extent that reduced her culpability. This combination of factors led to her long obsession with the belief that as his mother she owed a duty to Thomas to end his suffering. And there is no doubt about the genuineness of her belief that her actions in preparing for and eventually killing Thomas represented an act of mercy or that the grief consequent on the loss of her son is undiminished by her responsibility for his death. These are powerful considerations, far removed from the ordinary case of murder.

However the appellant's culpability is reduced, it is not extinguished. She had resolved to kill Thomas within a very short time of the accident, almost in its immediate aftermath, and well before the long-term results of the operations and treatment could be known, and *indeed while the remaining members of Thomas's family were still hoping that he would survive. She was convinced that she, and she alone, knew what was best for Thomas, to such an obsessive extent that any view to the contrary, however it was expressed, was to be rejected out of hand. This was not a moment or two of isolated thinking, but a settled intention. She tried to kill Thomas and did eventually kill him without a thought to the feelings of anyone else, including his father and his brothers, and indeed the members of the medical professions who were doing their very best to care for him. What is more, she assumed that she knew what Thomas's wishes would have been, and close as the bond between mother and son no doubt was, he was an adult whose mother would not always have been able to speak for him. When the first attempt failed, she ignored the potential consequence to others of denying her involvement in the offence, justifying the possibility that blame might pass unfairly to anyone else on the basis that she must continue to be free to achieve her objective. The process of preparing for trial for attempted murder, and the intimation that there would be a guilty plea, obscured the fact that she was making arrangements to deceive those responsible for her son's care into believing she was not his mother. And perhaps most significantly of all, her unsuccessful attempt to kill Thomas produced a deterioration in his condition without which, as far as we can see, the possibility of the withdrawal of hydration and nutrition would have been most unlikely to arise. In short, harsh as it is to have to say it, she had contributed to the very sorry condition from which, on the day of his death, Thomas was suffering, as well as the risk of the awful death from which she intended to relieve him. Because of her early fixed obsession, she never sought advice or information from medical experts on how the suffering of the patient might be reduced if the decision was made to apply to the court to allow him to die. As it is, her intention that Thomas should die was fixed long before that sad final state was reached because, as far as she was concerned, within a very short time of the accident, Thomas had to die. At that time no one else shared her view, and she decided that she must kill him herself. On the first occasion she failed to kill him, but added to his disabilities, and, on the second she was better prepared, and succeeded. We cannot allow any discount for a guilty plea (because there was none).*

This case involves one of the most difficult sentencing decisions faced in this court. We cannot interfere with the mandatory sentence of life imprisonment. Having reflected on all the relevant considerations, we

Criminal Justice

have decided that the minimum term ordered by the trial judge should be reduced to a period of 5 years.'

[2010] EWCA Crim 2637.
This information is licensed under the Open Government Licence.

Commentary

So the court imposed the mandatory sentence of life imprisonment, and Mrs English was required to spend five years in prison. The injustice in this tragic case lies at the door of the UK Parliament which created a mandatory sentence of life imprisonment for all cases of murder. This means that Mrs English will carry the public label of 'murderer' and remain under the court's order for the rest of her life. That seems unjust. Many scholars and practitioners have called for Parliament to remove the mandatory element of the sentence, and this case is a good example of why this reform is necessary.

The Court has written a lengthy and thoughtful judgment and imposed a term of custody which is shorter than the minimum term handed down in most cases of murder. Cases like this make the conventional analyses of aggravation and mitigation rather complicated. Committing a crime against a helpless or incapacitated victim is normally an aggravating factor, and the Court of Appeal noted this. But his helpless and vegetative state was the reason that Mrs English felt she needed to end his life, which rather sidelines the aggravating factor, I would have thought. Similarly, the Court noted that 'she never felt any sense of guilt or remorse'. True, but it would be unreasonable in this case to expect remorse when the defendant only committed the crime to spare the victim further suffering. The courts are required to apply the law, but some people may ask what, ultimately, is gained by putting Mrs English in prison for five years—beyond ensuring that some kind of public statement is made for the benefit of society. How are we better off as a society by paying hundreds of thousands of pounds to incarcerate this woman for five years? Can we not devise some other means of marking the wrongfulness of her conduct other than through the use of the prison?

Further reading

In light of the fact that criminal justice varies significantly around the world, it is hard to suggest readings which are not jurisdiction-specific. Despite its title, the *Oxford Handbook of Criminology* (given later in this section) contains a number of important chapters on criminal justice, while the series 'Crime and Justice' edited by Michael Tonry and published by the University of Chicago Press is an excellent source of 'state of the art' reviews of research on many topical subjects in criminal justice. In addition, the following readings offer some general analysis for three countries and thereafter I have suggested some key readings for each specific chapter.

Country-specific readings

Australia: Findlay, M., Odgers, S., and Yeo, S. (2014) *Australian Criminal Justice*. Oxford: Oxford University Press.

Canada: Roberts, J. V. and Grossman, M. (2015) (eds.) *Criminal Justice in Canada*. Toronto: Thomson Nelson.

UK: Hucklesby, A. and Wahidin, A. (2013) *Criminal Justice*. Oxford: Oxford University Press.

US/UK: Hirschel, D., Wakefield, W., and Sasse, S. (2006) *Criminal Justice in England and the U.S.* London: Jones and Bartlett.

General readings

Maguire, M. and Morgan, R. (2012) *Oxford Handbook of Criminology*. Oxford: Oxford University Press.

Pakes, F. (2014) *Comparative Criminal Justice*. London: Routledge.

Reiner, R. (2007) *Law and Order: An Honest Citizen's Guide to Crime and Control*. Cambridge: Polity Press.

Roberts, J. V. and Hough, M. (2005) *Understanding Public Attitudes to Criminal Justice*. Maidenhead: Open University Press.

Tonry, M. (2011) Crime and Criminal Justice. In: *Oxford Handbook of Crime and Criminal Justice*. New York: Oxford University Press.

Chapter 1: Introducing criminal justice

Huff, R. and Killias, M. (2013) *Wrongful Convictions and Miscarriages of Justice*. New York: Routledge.

Lab, S. (2008) Crime Prevention. In: S. Shoham, O. Beck, and M. Kett (eds.) *International Handbook of Penology and Criminal Justice*. New York: Taylor & Francis.

Zedner, L. (2004) *Criminal Justice*. Oxford: Oxford University Press.

Chapter 2: Between the crime and the court

McCoy, C. (2011) Prosecution. In: *Oxford Handbook of Crime and Criminal Justice*. New York: Oxford University Press.

Newburn, T. (2008) *Handbook of Policing*. Cullompton: Willan.

Sherman, L. (2011) Police and Crime Control. In: *Oxford Handbook of Crime and Criminal Justice*. New York: Oxford University Press.

Chapter 3: In court and on trial

Hastie, R., Penrod, S., and Pennington, S. (2013) *Inside the Jury*. London: The Lawbook Exchange.

Pizzi, W. (2008) A Comparative Look at the Prosecution and Defense in Western Trial Systems. In: *International Handbook of Penology and Criminal Justice*. New York: Taylor & Francis.

Nolan, J. (2012) Problem-Solving Courts. In: *Oxford Handbook of Sentencing and Corrections*. New York: Oxford University Press.

Chapter 4: Why punish . . . and how?

Ashworth, A. (2015) *Sentencing and Criminal Justice* (Sixth edition). Cambridge: Cambridge University Press.

Brooks, T. (2012) *Punishment*. London: Routledge.

Roberts, J. V. (2011) (ed.) *Mitigation and Aggravation at Sentencing*. Cambridge: Cambridge University Press.

Further reading

von Hirsch, A., Ashworth, A., and Roberts, J. V. (2009) (eds.) *Principled Sentencing: Readings on Theory and Policy*. Oxford: Hart Publishing.

Chapter 5: In and out of prison

Harding, R. (2012) Regulating Prison Conditions. In: *Oxford Handbook of Sentencing and Corrections*. New York: Oxford University Press.

Jewkes, Y. (2007) (ed.) *Handbook on Prisons*. Cullompton: Willan.

Rhine, E. (2012) The Present Status and Future Prospects of Parole. In: *Oxford Handbook of Sentencing and Corrections*. New York: Oxford University Press.

Chapter 6: Hearing the crime victim?

Bottoms, A. and Roberts, J. V. (2010) (eds.) *Hearing the Victim*. Cullompton: Willan.

Davis, R., Lurigio, A., and Herman, S. (2013) (eds.) *Victims of Crime*. London: Sage.

Walklate, S. (2007) *Handbook of Victims and Victimology*. London: Routledge.

Chapter 7: The future of criminal justice

Faulkner, D. and Burnett, R. (2012) *Where Next for Criminal Justice?* Bristol: The Policy Press.

Index

SOCIAL MEDIA
Very Short Introduction

Join our community

www.oup.com/vsi

- Join us online at the official Very Short Introductions Facebook page.
- Access the thoughts and musings of our authors with our online blog.
- Sign up for our monthly e-newsletter to receive information on all new titles publishing that month.
- Browse the full range of Very Short Introductions online.
- Read extracts from the Introductions for free.
- Visit our library of Reading Guides. These guides, written by our expert authors will help you to question again, why you think what you think.
- If you are a teacher or lecturer you can order inspection copies quickly and simply via our website.

ONLINE
CATALOGUE
A Very Short Introduction

Our online catalogue is designed to make it easy to find your ideal Very Short Introduction. View the entire collection by subject area, watch author videos, read sample chapters, and download reading guides.

http://fds.oup.com/www.oup.co.uk/general/vsi/index.html

FORENSIC PSYCHOLOGY
A Very Short Introduction
David Canter

Lie detection, offender profiling, jury selection, insanity in the law, predicting the risk of re-offending, the minds of serial killers and many other topics that fill news and fiction are all aspects of the rapidly developing area of scientific psychology broadly known as Forensic Psychology. *Forensic Psychology: A Very Short Introduction* discusses all the aspects of psychology that are relevant to the legal and criminal process as a whole. It includes explanations of criminal behaviour and criminality, including the role of mental disorder in crime, and discusses how forensic psychology contributes to helping investigate the crime and catching the perpetrators.